How to Start a Knife Sharpening Business

The Complete Guide to Starting Your Own Business Sharpening Knives, Scissors, Axes, Chisels and More!

BE THE BOSS ACADEMY

BE THE BOSS
ACADEMY

DISCLAIMER

The information you find in this book is not meant to replace professional advice and support offered by a career coach, investor, or similar expert. The data in this book are up to date at the time of writing, and the author undergoes significant research to provide accurate and actionable information. However, the author does not take responsibility for any losses or damage incurred by following the information that is made available in this book. Readers use any details shared in this book at their own risk.

CONTENTS

INTRODUCTION

"If you want good roses, sharpen your knife and harden your heart." - Patience Strong

How many sharp knives do you have in your kitchen? The truth is, a lot of people actually have many blunt knives. You only notice this when you're trying to cut through that perfect piece of steak, or perhaps when you want to cut up a few pieces of corn to place on the grill.

Before you get to this point, the idea of sharpening your knives might not have crossed your mind. They've been working so far, right? Well, truth is, knives get blunt over time. And this actually brings about an excellent opportunity for you to make some money - once you learn a bit more about sharpening knives, and maybe even other blades.

When discussing business opportunities with people, you'd often find that they are leaning toward health, fitness, investment, and similar industries. Those who rather enjoy working with their hands, however, might start to think out of the box and considered opportunities that aren't really so "generic". This may lead you to a knife-sharpening business - quite a turn-around from the regular business idea, right?

The thing is, this is a fast-growing industry that a lot of people overlook. And when you're able to find one of these industries, you have potential on your hands.

It might sound like a strange market to enter, but the truth is, it's underutilized, yet something that a lot of people are really interested in. And the thing is, it really matched the fact that many people generally enjoy working with their hands.

However, when it comes to looking at these business opportunities, it's really important that we narrow down the statistics. No matter how wonderful an idea is, you have to always ensure there's a market that l want your products or services.

Between 2021 and 2028, the knife sharpening service market in the United States is expected to grow by 6.5% annually. By 2028, this market is also estimated to reach a value of $117.1 million - and remember, these statistics only apply to the United States. In terms of employment, the average person who performs knife sharpening services is paid $22.14 per hour, with an annual salary of $46,040 (Mean).

Remember that this data is related to employees. Now, imagine you are the business owner - that means you'll be able to charge even more than this and keep the profits. Sure, it's possible to expand, but when you're just getting started, this should give you a good idea of what is possible.

If you've ever wanted to delve into the business of knife sharpening, you might not be sure where to start - and this is exactly where this guide comes into the picture. This book is going to talk more about how sharpening services work, the tools you need, and give you a good overview of what it takes to start this kind of business.

We'll also explore a step-by-step system that you can use to get going. This system uses seven expertly crafted steps that you have to follow in order.

Throughout the book, you'll also learn more about how you

can figure out the right pricing model for your services and decide on a sub-niche that you are going to target. We're also going to focus on ways that you can still offer this service if your budget doesn't immediately allow for the purchase of professional machines.

Many people have already been able to achieve great levels of success when it comes to a knife-sharpening business.

One of the best examples that we can share here is The American Edge. Just one person started this business, and it has really taken off. The business was started eight years ago. By 2018, Matt Rowell, the owner and founder, earned up to $500 per month. He's been able to scale this business to earn him an extra $1,500 per month.

Of course, he continues to work on the project alone, and he didn't decide to scale up too much - but even just $1,500 extra in your bank account every month can be incredibly useful.

So, with that success story out of the way, let's turn our focus to you - you're looking to reach into your inner entrepreneur. By the end of this book, you'll be equipped with everything you need to start your own knife-sharpening business.

You'll understand what you need to get started with the business, and the equipment you require, and you'll even have knowledge about different sharpening techniques that you can use. Plus, we'll also help you create a process that works for you, and show you how you can market your knife sharpening services so that it is seen by those who need this service.

CHAPTER 1
SHARPENING YOUR MINDSET

When it comes to starting a business, your mindset plays a critical role in whether or not you're going to achieve success. If you don't work on your mindset beforehand, you might end up with little motivation. That's going to make you more likely to give up halfway through, never actually reaching the point where you can say, "I've successfully opened my knife sharpening services to the public."

Now, when it comes to a sharpening business, you have to understand that it's not for everyone. That's why, before we dive deeper into what a sharpening business is all about and how you can be successful in this market, you're first going to have to decide if it's the right business model for you.

Don't fret, though. There are a lot of people who are a good fit for a sharpening business. The main thing you have to consider is the fact that you're going to have to work with your hands. If

1

that's not something that seems off-putting to you, then a sharpening business might be just what you're looking for.

THE GREAT THING about this business model is the fact that it has a high demand. Have you recently invested in a new set of knives? You probably found that it's much more expensive than a few years ago. Prices are going up - and that includes the cost of quality knives. As prices for these items increase, the demand for sharpening services also starts to rise. That's because people are more likely to invest in sharpening services than spend hundreds of dollars to get a new set of knives.

THERE ARE other factors that also contribute to the increased demand for sharpening services. While it's true that DIY sharpeners are available, they often have limitations, can only be used for specific types of objects, and people don't necessarily know how to use them properly.

COOKING shows are also contributing to more people choosing to cook at home. It's easy to put on a YouTube video and follow along. It gives people a chance to feel like they are a chef in their own kitchen - and with this comes an increased demand for sharp knives at home.

SURE, you're going to have to overcome some challenges, but by taking a look at these figures and being someone who doesn't mind working with their hands - you have a profitable business opportunity at your disposal. In this chapter, we're going to take a closer look at how you can adopt a successful entrepreneurial mindset, and also consider what it really takes to begin your own sharpening business.

THE MINDSET OF A SUCCESSFUL ENTREPRENEUR

No matter what kind of business you're planning to start, the right mindset makes a big difference - and it's also one of the very first things that you have to focus on. So, with that set, let's start by taking a closer look at the mindset of a successful entrepreneur. The good news here is that there are a lot of successful entrepreneurs who have spoken up not only about the challenges they have faced, but also about the type of mindset they had to adopt. We can really learn from them and take what they have shared with us - then use that to our advantage.

BEFORE WE GO DEEPER into this type of mindset, I want you to take a closer look at a list of traits that are often associated with successful entrepreneurs:

- Being open to new possibilities
- Being able to see the positive even in negative situations
- Being curious and creative
- Being able to effectively persuade
- Being able to motivate yourself without the need for external motivators
- Being able to take lead, be resilient, and not let small things linger in your mind
- Being able to put and see yourself in someone else's shoes (or perspective)

THIS LIST DOESN'T COVER every single trait, but it's a good start. Here's the thing, being a successful entrepreneur or, at least in this case, having the right mindset, doesn't mean you have to be able to tick off every box here. If you have a couple of these traits, then you're already at an advantage. The ones you don't have - those are things you can equip yourself with.

WITH THIS IN MIND, there are a couple of things that you will need if you're going to be successful with your own sharpening business - particularly in terms of mindset. We're going to cover those in this section, and if you don't have these mindset traits, it's important that you start working on them.

- **Growth Mindset:** You need to make sure you adopt a mindset that focuses on growth. While it's incredibly important to live in the moment and be aware of what's going on right now, you also have to make sure to consider the future and how your business can continue to grow. That way, you won't limit yourself to growth. Instead, you'll constantly be exploring opportunities to rise up and push your business to new heights. Sure, when you're a sole proprietor, then it might be tough to grow big - but it's always still helpful to get more clients and expose your business to a greater number of potential buyers.

THIS ONE MIGHT BE a tricky factor for some people. If you're used to just focusing on now, and you find yourself afraid of thinking about how you could grow in the next six months or maybe a year, there are ways to adopt a growth mindset. The first step is really to embrace what's going on and to get to know yourself better. Then, you'll have to adopt a positive mindset.

- **Ability to Take Risks:** The next thing you need to take note of is your ability to take risks. Now, this doesn't mean risking it all when the signs of failure are clear. Instead, it's the ability to assess risks and decide which ones are worth opting for.

UNCERTAINTY IS something that you're going to face at some point when you run a business. Being able to navigate through uncertain times and understand which way to go is important. However, you also have to understand which decisions are going to come with how much risk - and then, make an informed choice in terms of what you are going to do. At the same time, you shouldn't be able to take these risks. Holding back and delaying just because you're afraid of risks can not only be costly in the long run but also seriously limit your ability to grow. Essentially, you need to be able to take risks, but you also have to make sure you are able to assess the risk that you're taking at the same time.

- **Perseverance:** No matter what kind of business you're looking to start, being able to persevere is incredibly important. And this may apply even more to businesses in the sharpening industry. That's because you're going to face challenges, and the competition may even be stiff at times, depending on where you live and the audience you're targeting.

WHEN THINGS START to look tough, you need to be able to push through. That's exactly where perseverance comes into the picture. It's the ability to understand the position you're in right

5

now, but also to see that it's possible to get through a rut and come out at the top. This is a skill that's going to make sure you don't get stuck in a difficult situation, but instead, know that if you keep going, things can turn around in the future.

- **Vision:** You also need to have a vision for your business. If you're completely new to the business of knife sharpening, then this specific step may be somewhat of a challenge. However, it doesn't mean you cannot develop a solid vision for the business that you're looking to start.

IT STARTS with understanding yourself and the type of business you want to start - in this case, it's going to be a knife-sharpening business. Now, the "vision" part of an entrepreneurial mindset doesn't just focus on a specific type of business. It's also something that can apply to a more general situation, where you have the ability to create a vision for yourself, regardless of what you want to accomplish.

- **Passion:** Another important trait or skill that we want to focus on here is passion. If you start a business in a niche that you have no passion for, then you're going to have a tough time staying motivated. We tend to be more motivated and feel a greater sense of inspiration when targeting a business niche that we have a passion for - so that's definitely something to keep in mind.

PASSION FOR A SPECIFIC NICHE, however, is not the only factor that you need to keep in mind here. You also have to make sure you have a passion for running your own business, being a leader, and taking charge in general. These are also things that will surely be useful when it comes to getting started.

IN TERMS of a knife sharpening business, it would definitely be useful if you have a passion for working with your hands. There's not a lot of hard labor involved, especially if you're able to invest in machinery that can sharpen knives, axes, and other tools - but it's still a job that requires some manual labor from your side.

WHAT IT TAKES TO START A SHARPENING BUSINESS

Now that we've taken a closer look at what type of mindset you need when it comes to starting a business and being a successful entrepreneur, it's important that we also cover a few necessities for a sharpening business in particular.

THERE ARE a couple of things that we need to discuss in this section, including the technical skills you need, business skills, and some of the obstacles that you'll likely need to overcome if you want to be successful. We'll also cover the important role that consistent learning plays in helping you not only start but also run a successful, sharpening business.

TECHNICAL SKILLS

Let's start with a couple of technical skills that you'll need when you want to start this type of business. As you can imagine, your main job will basically be to sharpen knives, axes, scissors, and other sharp tools that your customers often work with. You need to be able to use the right tools in order to sharpen these blades.

If you don't have the necessary technical skills, you're going to have a tough time delivering a quality and satisfactory experience to your customers - and this can be bad for business.

THUS, it's a good idea to equip yourself with the necessary knowledge and technical skills before you move on to other aspects of a sharpening business. There are many ways to learn how all of this works. For example, you could buy a few pieces of equipment needed to sharpen blades, then follow some tutorials or guides. You can go onto YouTube for some tutorials - there are actually a couple of experts who share details about how these tools work and how you can effectively sharpen the edges of different blades. Alternatively, see if there are any in-person courses offered in your local area. This can be a good idea if you prefer a more hands-on learning experience as opposed to reading text-based tutorials or watching videos

THE MAIN THING here is to ensure you know how to use different blade-sharpening equipment. You also have to understand things like the right angle to use when sharpening a blade, as incorrect positioning can cause serious damage to items that your client brings you. You don't want to end up damaging a knife set that's going to put your business in the red when you have to replace it, after all.

ONCE YOU EQUIP yourself with these skills, you can start to look at the next steps - which include understanding how businesses work and how you should start and manage your own company.

BUSINESS SKILLS

Next up - business skills. Even if you're really skilled with knife sharpening, if you don't have the necessary business skills, then you'll have a tough time getting your business running and keeping it successful.

THERE ARE a couple of things that you need to consider when it comes to business skills. Thus, let's take a quick look at some of the business skills that you need to equip yourself with to be successful:

- **Formalities and legalities:** You need to understand the fact that there are different kinds of business structures. Not every structure is the same. Some have obvious advantages over others, but each structure still has its own pros and cons. Being able to recognize the most ideal type of business structure for your company is critical. Additionally, you also need to understand the legal factors that come into play when starting your business, even if you're planning to run it from home.
- **Finding clients:** Your ability to find clients that are willing to pay for your services will also play a big role in the success of your business. You need to equip yourself with marketing skills and understand where you're going to find clients that can help your business grow.
- **Pricing your services:** It's not just about finding the right clients, but also about understanding how you should price your services. If you're too expensive, then potential clients are going to turn to your competitors. On the other hand, if your prices are too

low, you might find yourself losing money instead of turning a profit. You need the ability to thoroughly research your competitors and decide on a price that's attractive and profitable.

- **Scaling your business:** As your business grows, there comes a time when you should consider expanding and scaling up. This is actually another business skill you need - the ability to recognize when you should start to consider scaling up.
- **Dealing with taxes:** When it comes to legalities, you also have to understand not only how to manage the finances of your business but also the taxes. Make sure you know how business taxes work for the specific type of company that you're starting, and then fill out your taxes and pay them on time at the correct intervals. This helps to ensure your business doesn't need to worry about stepping over legal lines.

UNDERSTANDING AND OVERCOMING OBSTACLES

No matter the type of business you want to start, there will always be obstacles that you're going to face along the way. Knowing what type of obstacles there are with a sharpening business, as well as how you can overcome them, plays a critical role in ensuring long-term success.

One of the biggest challenges that you may face is not believing in yourself. This is a hurdle that may be especially difficult to overcome early on. If you don't believe in yourself, then you're going to have trouble with issues like poor self-confidence - which is something you really need when it comes to getting your business going, working with clients, and seeing the light even when things start to seem dark.

. . .

ANOTHER OBSTACLE IS HARD TIMES. If you face a situation where things seem dire, are you going to give up or continue striving for success? That's something that can also make or break your business in the long run. You need to be resilient if you're going to overcome this particular obstacle.

NEVER STOP LEARNING

Above all, one of the most important things that you need to do when starting and running a business is to continue learning. Once you've gone through some educational material on running a business and you've equipped yourself with the skills you need to sharpen blades - that's not the end of your learning journey. Instead, rather think of it as a beginning.

THE THING that you need to keep in mind here is that the world around us is changing consistently. That means you have to make sure you adapt to these changes. And to do that, you're going to have to continue learning and striving toward greater things. That means adopting the latest techniques for sharpening, as well as constantly assessing your business strategies and comparing it to what the norm is at that very moment.

SUMMARY / Key Takeaways

- While there is money to be made with a knife-sharpening business, it's important to understand that it's not for everyone. You need to be willing to work with your hands and to adopt the right sharpening skills for this type of business model.
- However, if you're willing to put in the necessary effort, then it's going to be a profitable business to

start. The rates of knives and other sharp objects is going up along with prices for many other items people use in their daily lives - so it becomes more viable to have them sharpened instead of buying new ones.

- To get started, you have to equip yourself with the appropriate technical skills. That also means knowing how to work with different sharpening tools. Additionally, make sure you become business-savvy, as that's going to make sure you're able to start and run a company that is successful.
- Apart from all this, being passionate about your business is another requirement you shouldn't overlook. If you're passionate about this type of task (blade sharpening, working with your hands), then it's a great business idea!

WE'VE COVERED some of the basics, and now, it's time to get started with your business idea. But, first, you need to understand how sharpening works - so, in the next chapter, we're going to take a closer look at how you can sharpen knives, even by hand.

CHAPTER 2

SHARPENING 101

Before you jump into things like your business plan and setting things up, it's a good idea to first equip yourself with the skills to properly sharpen knives, scissors, and other objects with blades. Now, you could choose to niche down into a specific category, such as only working with knives. However, it's still useful to make sure you have more general knowledge, as it can be helpful not only during the beginning but also as you scale your company.

So, in this chapter, we're taking a closer look at a few basics related to sharpening. Think of this as an introduction to sharpening and a way to develop some initial skills. Once you equip yourself with these skills, you can continue with the rest of the steps you need to take when starting a business.

HERE's the thing - even if you've never sharpened a knife before, there's no need to worry. It's actually not a difficult skill to equip yourself with. Follow along and consider getting some basic equipment to start practicing. After all, practice makes perfect!

HOW EDGES BECOME SHARP

One of the most important things that you need to understand when it comes to sharpening is the edges. Now, there's some science to all of this. You see, the edge of a knife, pair of scissors, or an axe essentially determines just how sharp that object is. In scientific terms, an edge is described as the point where two surfaces touch - or come into contact. It's also sometimes referred to as the contact area - and that's what you'll be focusing on when you sharpen objects.

THERE ARE different ways to sharpen an edge on objects like knives and scissors, but you have to make sure you always keep this scientific element in mind. The size of that contact point is what will essentially determine the sharpness, but, at the same time, there are cases where the surfaces that lead toward the contact point shouldn't be too thin.

THINK OF AN AXE, for example. It has a very small contact point, which ensures it can effectively penetrate wood as you chop. However, the rest of the axe's blade is relatively thick. Things are different with a knife, however. While there are different kinds of knives on the market, you'll usually notice that the entire blade has a relatively thin structure - especially when you compare it to objects like axes.

REGARDLESS, the idea here is to use grinding tools to wear down parts of the two surfaces that form the contact point. You'll generally want to do this at an angle, as that helps to create a contact point that is as small as possible - something that's really important when it comes to sharpening blades.

WHAT YOU NEED TO SHARPEN A KNIFE

Now that you have a better understanding of the role that an edge plays in sharpening, it's crucial to ensure you know about the specific tools and things you need. Having the right equipment and tools plays an important role when it comes to being effective at this job. With this said you should note that what you need does depend on the type of blades that you're going to sharpen. Some people may decide to start out by only sharpening some of the more basic bladed objects, like knives. This way, you'll essentially limit the variety of tools and hardware you need in order to sharpen objects. As you grow your business, you can start to expand and offer your customers more options to sharpen other objects.

ONE OF THE best starting points here is a sharpening stone. The great thing about a sharpening stone is the fact that it is relatively inexpensive and can do really well when it comes to sharpening blades. Now, you have to understand that there are a couple of options available when looking at sharpening stones. You get synthetic ones, as well as whetstones. Synthetic stones are usually made from abrasive particles - that's going to help you wear down some of the material on the surfaces that lead to the edge of the blade.

WHEN IT COMES to buying a sharpening stone, you're going to have to focus on the grit rating. This is actually quite similar to the grit ratings you can see when buying sandpaper. It essentially tells you how abrasive the specific stone is. This will affect the amount of material you're able to remove from the side surfaces that you need to grind in order to create a sharper edge.

APART FROM A SHARPENING STONE, there is also the need to add a polished look to a knife after you're done with the process itself. This is where a strop becomes really handy. There are different types available, but if you're just getting started with sharpening, then opt for a basic one that isn't too expensive. This can help you add a nice finishing touch to the blades you're going to sharpen without adding too much to the initial expense you have to cover when starting out.

ANOTHER THING that you should consider getting is a wet towel. You can generally use a standard towel. The main idea here is to have an object that can help to keep the stone in place while you use it to sharpen a blade. If the stone moves around, it's going to be difficult to get good results, and you might end up causing damage to a blade instead of creating a new, sharper edge.

NOTE that these are the basics. It's a great starting point, and as you get some clients and you focus on growing your business, you can then begin to look at other tools that can streamline the process. For example, there are machines with moving sharpening stones that are automatically kept in place. These are more expensive hardware but will likely prove useful when you have some extra income that you can spend on business-related elements.

HOW TO SHARPEN A KNIFE BY HAND

Now that we've covered some of the essentials you need to start sharpening knives and considered the important role of understanding how edges on blades work let's take a closer look at how to actually do it.

IN THIS SECTION, we're going to primarily focus on sharpening knives. However, you'll use similar techniques when you need to sharpen other types of blades, such as those on axes or scissors.

WITH THAT SAID, here is a step-by-step process that you can use to help you practice knife sharpening:

1. **Bevel:** The first step is to choose the bevel that you're going to use. Now, this step may be a little complicated if you're not experienced, so the 50/50 bevel is a really good starting point. The majority of knives that you use in your kitchen use this bevel, and it's also one of the more common options. It means the edge or contact point will be positioned exactly at the center of the blade. Carefully inspect the edge of the blade before you decide on a bevel, as there are specialty knives and other sharp objects that require a different technique.

2. **Secure Grip:** When you're sharpening knives, you will be working with very sharp blades. That means you have to focus on your safety throughout the entire process. One particularly important factor that helps to ensure you are safe is to make sure you have a secure and proper grip on the handle of the knife. A secure grip will also help to give you better results while sharpening.

3. **The Right Angle:** The angle at which you hold the knife will play a big role in how well of a job you're going to do. When you're just getting started, it's a

good idea to use a 20-degree angle. It's a standard angle that works for a wide variety of blade types. It also gives you a good angle to remove some of the surface on the sides of the knife, which helps to create that perfectly sharp contact point. Try to keep the knife in the same angle while sharpening. You should also use the same angle for both sides of the blade.

4. **Burr:** As you continue to make even strokes on your sharpening stone, you'll start to notice what experts call the burr. That's when it seems like the edge you're working on is beginning to curl to the opposite side. Once you reach the burr, it's time to switch to the other side of the blade. You'll begin to alternate between the two sides up to the point where there is no longer a burr. At this point, the knife is sharp.

You CAN NOW REPEAT this process as many times as you need until the knife is sharp enough according to your expectations. To test the sharpness, get a piece of paper and make a cut. If you get a clean cut, then the blade is likely sharp enough. If you're working with a blade that is very blunt, then you'll likely need to repeat this process multiple times to get it sharp again. However, the grit type that you use will also play a role in deciding how long it will take to properly sharpen the blade. If you do find that the current grit doesn't work well, you can opt for a sharpening stone with a more abrasive grit - but move up on the grit level slowly so that you don't cause damage to the blade.

IF YOU'RE GOING to be using a strop, then use it once you're satisfied with the sharpness of the blade. They're relatively easy to use and will help to add a polished look to the knife, while also helping to remove any more debris that might have collected on the surface of the blade during the sharpening process.

DIFFERENT SHARPENING METHODS

Manual sharpening is a great way to get started. As we've mentioned previously, however, understanding there are more options available to streamline the sharpening process is also important. If you're working on a limited budget, then a sharpening stone and strop are good enough to get you going. However, when you start to see an increase in the number of people who use your services, you'll likely soon start to feel that the task gets tedious and repetitive. It's true that a sharpening stone gives you a much greater level of control over how you sharpen the blade compared to other methods, but it is a more labor-intensive task. It also takes longer to sharpen blades this way.

Now, let's turn our attention to some of the other sharpening methods that are also available. These might not be as beginner-friendly when you're just starting up, mostly due to the higher price tag. Later in this book, we're going to take a closer look at techniques you can use to grow your business. When you do focus on scaling up, you're going to want to invest in tools that can speed up the sharpening process.

THIS IS where electric sharpeners come into the picture. They don't give you as much control as a sharpening stone, but by the time you upgrade to this tool, you'll have gained the experience you need to use these tools more effectively. There are also manual and automatic rotating stones available, which can also give you a more streamlined process for sharpening blades.

• • •

SUMMARY / *Key Takeaways*

- Edges are the main focus point when it comes to sharpening blades. The contact point refers to the area where the two surfaces come into contact, and the smaller that point, the sharper the blade.
- You can start out with a sharpening stone. It gives you a great practice tool and can even be used for commercial purposes. Add a strop if you want to polish knives and other blades once you have sharpened them.
- When sharpening knives by hand, focus on the bevel, use the right angle, and make sure you've got a good grip on the knife's handle.
- Over time, you can consider scaling up, growing your business, and equipping yourself with better tools that make the sharpening process faster and more diverse.

YOU SHOULD NOW HAVE A BETTER idea about how knife sharpening works. Once you practice a bit and start to get more acquainted with how it works, it's time to move on. In the next chapter, we're going to take a look at the specific tools and steps that you need to start your own sharpening business.

CHAPTER 3

TAKING A STAB AT YOUR OWN KNIFE SHARPENING BUSINESS, STEP-BY-STEP

You now have a better idea about what it takes to start your own knife sharpening business. Maybe you've even followed my advice and practiced sharpening on a stone. The main thing that I want you to understand here is that anyone can really start a knife-sharpening business. You don't need to be an expert in the field. As you've already discovered, it's actually quite a straightforward process to sharpen knives, as well as other types of blades, even by hand.

THE NEXT STEP is to understand what you need to do in order to start a knife-sharpening business. Using a step-by-step system is going to give you better results, which is exactly what we're going to do here. In this chapter, I'll quickly go through some of the most vital steps that you'll need to take when starting a sharpening business. In the upcoming chapters, I'll expand on each of these points to give you a more in-depth view of everything you should do.

STEP 1: CARVE OUT YOUR NICHE

The first thing you may think when we talk about the niche is that a sharpening business is already a niche on its own. That's true, but you have to understand that there are sub-niches. When you filter down to one of those more targeted niches, you're giving yourself a number of advantages.

THIS STARTS with the fact that you'll be able to target customers more effectively. When you decide to only sharpen axes, for example, you won't be targeting the average consumer who uses knives in their kitchen. Instead, you'll be targeting wood choppers - including businesses that have employees who chop up wood or chop down trees.

THE MAIN IDEA here is to consider the specific types of blades that you want to focus on with your sharpening business. While you can decide to expand to more blade types over time to offer a greater level of diversity, starting out with more specific elements can be helpful in the beginning.

IT'S important to do some research to determine what kind of niche you should target when it comes down to a sharpening business. That starts with looking at your competitors. Consider other sharpening businesses in your local area, as this will give you a good idea of who you're up against. Take note of the specific services they offer. It can be useful to choose a sub-niche that's not readily available in your local area. In that case, you're going to fill a gap. However, you do need to make sure there is a high demand for that type of sharpening service. Offering axe sharpening services in an area where trees and wood are not really a daily sight, for example, would not be a good idea.

. . .

YOU SHOULD SPEND some time on this one. That's because the niche you choose will play a big part in how successful you're going to be. Choose the right niche, and you're setting a strong foundation to work from for yourself.

STEP 2: DECIDE WHICH SERVICES TO OFFER

You're going to start a sharpening business, so you might think this step is worth skipping. However, it's still important to sit down and list the specific services that you want to offer your customers. Not only should you decide on the services you'll offer, but you also have to consider what you're not going to provide in terms of services.

KEEP in mind the specific niche that you've decided to go after. Additionally, you also have to consider what type of equipment you have available. These are things that will help you decide on the services you should offer.

FOR EXAMPLE, if you're going to start out with just a sharpening stone, you'll notice that it's not the best tool for scissors and axes. Thus, your service list may include sharpening knives, and exclude sharpening axes or scissors. Thus, when a customer comes to you, you'll know when to tell them that you are unable to help them with their needs. While you don't necessarily want to show potential business away, it's also important to know when you won't be able to deliver on the expectations of a customer. This could well save you from a bad review.

STEP 3: SET YOUR PRICES

Knowing how much you're going to charge for your services while planning things out is another important step to take. This process will also require some research, as you'll need to take a closer look at what your competitors are charging for sharpening services. Additionally, you have to take into consideration factors like the time it takes you to sharpen knives and other blades, the cost of your equipment, and other expenses that you need to cover.

WHEN YOU TAKE ALL of these factors into consideration, then you're going to have an easier time determining the right prices to use for your services. You could also use a strategy where you offer base services, packages, and add-ons.

FOR EXAMPLE, you could set a base price for knife sharpening. Then, you have an add-on like polishing, and it comes at a small extra fee. You could also have a special price when someone needs you to sharpen an entire collection of knives. Of course, pricing can be more detailed, such as a specific rate based on the amount of time you spend or the type of knife that the client needs to be sharpened.

STEP 4: CREATE YOUR WORKSPACE

Having a good place to work when you're sharpening knives is another important matter that you shouldn't really overlook. Don't start your knife sharpening business without first focusing on this element. If you have a workspace, it's going to make things feel more organized.

. . .

YOU DON'T NECESSARILY NEED to throw everything out of the garage to set up a workspace. You simply need a dedicated spot where you can sharpen knives. Now, when starting a business, we often think that we need to rent out a building. However, with this type of business, you can actually start at home. There are some things to take into consideration when setting up your workspace in your home. For example, if there are pets or kids around, you have to pick a location where they won't be able to easily gain access to the knives and other blades you're working with - as it can be a hazard for them.

ONE IDEA WOULD BE to use your study or a spare room. Some people also find it useful to dedicate just a corner of their garage to their knife sharpening business. Since everyone's situation is unique, you're going to have to take a closer look at your living environment and then determine what would be a good choice for your workspace. The good thing about this step at the moment is the fact that you're just getting started. That means you're likely going to start out with just your basic sharpening stone, which doesn't require a lot of space. As your business grows and you are able to buy more hardware, you can start to consider how you will expand your workspace.

STEP 5: FIGURE OUT YOUR PROCESS

The next step is to determine the specific process you're going to use. This is actually a step that requires some experimentation from your side. It's a good idea to go to grab a few knives from your kitchen and go to your workspace. Sharpen a couple of these knives. Take a closer look at the specific process that you follow.

· · ·

THE MAIN IDEA here is to create a system that you can work on. When you've got this type of system, it's much easier to start offering your services to clients. It's not only going to help ensure you remain organized but can also be a big step in reducing the risk of errors - such as giving one client's knives to a different client.

YOUR PROCESS MAY INVOLVE specific steps. For example, when the client hands off their knives, you might start by adding their knives to a box and adding a label with the client's name or perhaps a reference number that you are going to work with. Next, you determine the order in which different knives need to be sharpened; then you go through the process.

OF COURSE, that's only one example of how you could develop a system that works well for you. It's also a good idea to document the actual steps you take during the sharpening process. That can become useful when you need a reference to work from later on - such as the type of bevel and the specific angle you used to achieve specific results.

STEP 6: FIND CUSTOMERS

Simply setting up a plan is not enough. Once you've got your workstation up and you have a specific process, it's time to start finding customers. It's a good idea to start out small. Try to promote your services to a few local people - this could even include family members or friends. During this time, taking only a few clients can help to give you more time to work with - that can be incredibly useful when you are still trying to experiment with your techniques and process.

· · ·

It's important to develop a marketing strategy that will help to expose your business to the right people. For this particular step, it's important to keep some of the previous decisions you made in mind. For example, take into consideration the niche that you're going to target and the services you want to offer. These are useful factors when it comes to determining who you should target with your campaigns and how you should go about promoting your business and services.

STEP 7: SCALE YOUR BUSINESS

Starting out small is a great way to build up some initial experience. You begin by promoting your services and then accepting client requests. Over time, however, you may want to scale things up. This is a good idea once you feel more comfortable with the entire knife sharpening process.

There are different ways to scale your business. It does come down to the progress you've been making, where you're working from, and the type of business model you decided to follow. Some options include hiring an employee or two. One employee could handle administrative tasks, while the other one can help you with the actual sharpening process. You've already gone through the process of teaching yourself how the sharpening process works, so now you can teach another employee. This will make sure you are able to increase the number of clients you can take on at the same time.

Another option when it comes to scaling up is to expand the workspace you have. In cases where you are seeing a significant level of success, this may even include hiring a workshop and buying equipment that can speed up the actual sharpening process. In this case, you'll have more space to work with. You could even consider getting multiple employees to help with the expansion of your business and to make sure you can continue scaling up without worrying about feeling overwhelmed as the number of clients starts to increase.

Now, while scaling up is a great way to aim for success, it's important to ensure you don't forget the original mission and vision you had for your business. Never lose sight of your roots - these roots are some of the things that can help build trust amongst people who are in need of sharpening services.

SUMMARY / *Key Takeaways*

- When it comes to starting your own knife sharpening business, following the seven-step system that we shared can give you a great way to begin. It's not only great for starting out, but this system is also going to help carry you as you continue serving clients and scaling your business.
- It's important to begin with the right niche, set competitive prices, and get a dedicated spot that you can call your workspace.
- Understanding how to attract and find clients is critical, as this serves as an important element in being successful with your knife-sharpening business. Then, as your client count grows, you can start to consider ways to scale up.

WE'VE BRIEFLY TOUCHED on each of the steps that are part of this seven-step system. In the following chapters, we're going to take a deeper dive into each of these steps and expand a bit more to help you better understand what you should do, and why they are important, and give you a look at the bigger picture.

CHAPTER 4

CARVE OUT YOUR NICHE

I f you do some research locally, you may find that there are a couple of knife sharpening businesses that you're going to go up against. Competition is something that you can't avoid, no matter what kind of business you're looking to start. However, take a closer look at each of these businesses. Compare them to each other. Something you'll notice is that they are quite different from each other. Even though the main idea remains the same, which is to offer sharpening services, there are often differences in terms of the services each business offers, how they go about the entire process, the marketing methods they use, and more.

THIS IS MAINLY because there are different niches within the sharpening industry. So, while one business might focus on sharpening knives, another one may have a more industrial focus, targeting businesses that work with larger blades. This is also where choosing your own niche comes into the picture. While we did briefly discuss the topic of niches in the previous chapter, we'd like to go into more detail about it in this chapter.

· · ·

THE MAJOR THING about choosing your niche is the fact that it's going to help you feel more organized. You'll also have a clearer vision for your business, as you know exactly what type of services you want to offer your clients. In this chapter, we're going to dive deeper into the niches related to knife sharpening, and I'm going to help you niche down so that you have a better vision of your business's purpose.

THE IMPORTANCE OF CHOOSING A NICHE

Some people may enter this entire business opportunity thinking that niching down isn't necessary. You're going to offer sharpening services, so that's specific enough. Right? Not really. The thing is, there are niches within the sharpening industry that you should understand. And by niching down, you're going to have an easier time actually finding the right target audience and promoting your services to them.

THE MAIN BENEFIT that comes with choosing a niche is the fact that it's easier to target customers. When you're going to offer sharpening services in general, it's hard to know who to target. There are residential and commercial customers, and even within these two categories, there are still sub-categories that you'll have to take into consideration.

IT'S DEFINITELY a good idea to take your own expertise and personal interests into account when you're trying to choose a niche within the sharpening business. For example, if you decide to target the average consumer who uses knives in their kitchen, you have a clear view of who you're targeting. That's going to make it easier to set up marketing campaigns. It also ensures you don't get customers who you are not able to serve.

· · ·

THE REASON you have to choose a niche right now is because it's going to be incredibly helpful later on. It's not just going to help you right now. In the long run, having a specific niche gives you a better view of how you can expand. It becomes really helpful when you decide to hire employees and expand, as you have a good idea about the vision for your business over time.

DIFFERENT NICHES IN THE SHARPENING WORLD

You have a better idea about the role that a niche plays in your sharpening business, but what niches are available? When you're just getting started, it's really challenging to thoroughly understand what niches are available within this industry. For many people, sharpening seems like a niche itself.

So, let's take a closer look at some of the specific niches that you're able to target if you want to start a sharpening business. This list will give you some clarity and should help you understand which direction you want to move in with your business specifically.

- **Consumer knives:** One of the major niches that you can focus on is consumer knives. This might actually also be one of the easier ones to enter, but you still have to consider how stiff the competition is in your local area. As the name suggests, you'll be focusing on sharpening standard knives that people use in their homes. Your focus point here would be on kitchen knives, for example. People use knives in their kitchen everyday, especially if they cook at home.

A LOT of people spend a significant amount of money when they invest in a high-quality knife set for their kitchen. Over time, especially with frequent usage, the edges on these knives start to become blunt. This makes it harder to chop vegetables and process meats while cooking.

IT'S MORE economical to get those knives sharpened compared to investing in an entirely new set. While people can find inexpensive sharpening objects at their local supermarket, they usually don't understand the techniques required to properly sharpen their knives. This is why they will turn to your business to get their knives professionally sharpened.

OF COURSE, when it comes to consumer knives, you can later expand into more categories. At first, you might focus on basic knives. As you start to make a profit, you can buy equipment that allows you to sharpen other consumer objects, such as scissors. This can help to expand on the specific services you offer customers and even give you new angles to target when setting up marketing plans.

- **Industrial knives:** Apart from your regular kitchen knives, there are also many industrial blades that need to be kept sharp. These blades can be used in both residential and commercial settings. Some examples of industrial options include the blades that are used in food processors, shears, and garden tools that are used to trim plants.

WHEN YOU DECIDE on industrial knives and blades as your niche, you get a relatively broad area to focus on. It's a good option if you don't want to have too many limitations on what you can offer your customers when you're getting started. However, it's also important to note that a simple sharpening stone may not be sufficient for some of the blades that you'll need to sharpen. Thus, you will likely need a bigger startup budget if you're going to target industrial blades since the equipment you need will cost more than what you require if you focus on kitchen knives, for example.

WITH THIS SAID, you can generally charge more for services that focus on industrial blades. That means it might be a more profitable niche in the long run, but it's also important to note that it's not as beginner-friendly as some of the other niches you can target when you start a sharpening business.

- **Axe heads:** While a large number of sharpening businesses will focus on knives, it's important to realize that there are other types of blades that need to be sharpened, too. This includes axe heads. It is possible to mix axe heads with another niche, but you may find that it's better to target it specifically when you are getting started. This is a good niche if you've got a particular interest in axes, woodcutting, and similar elements.

SIMILAR TO THE blades that you'll work with, if you decide to target industrial options with axe heads, you will need some special equipment. It's generally not a good idea to sharpen axe heads with a sharpening stone. Not only may this alter the accuracy of the sharpening, but it's also going to take a very long time to sharpen axe heads the manual way. Thus, you need a few tools that can automate and streamline the sharpening process. You'll also find that companies generally charge more for axe head sharpening compared to kitchen knives, so in the long run, it's a profitable niche.

IF YOU DECIDE to opt for axe heads, however, then you have to make sure you have the necessary skills. Axes are much larger than knives, and their unique shape sometimes makes it challenging to work with these tools. The angle and bevel you use to sharpen an axe are also relatively different when you compare them to knives. It's a niche that will require some practicing from your side before you begin to offer your services to customers. That will make sure you don't end up disappointing customers by damaging their axes or causing them to become even more blunt than they already are, instead of offering a new sharp edge when they pick up their axes.

- **B2B services:** You can also decide to offer B2B (business-to-business) services. In this case, you can still target specific types of blades, such as knives or axes. The difference here is the fact that you're not going to target the average consumer cooking in their kitchen. Instead, your focus will rather turn to businesses in your local area.

NOTE that there are many businesses that work with knives and other blades on a regular basis. Take restaurants as an example. They need sharp knives to ensure chefs who are responsible for preparing food can work efficiently in the kitchen. Thus, you can target this type of business - and this way, you'll give them a chance to ensure the knives that are available will always be sharp. Hairdressers can also be a good target for B2B services, as they work with scissors and blades while cutting or styling hair. It's incredibly important for hairdressers to always have sharp blades on hand, as that ensures they don't pull a client's hair during the cutting process. It also helps them give customers more accurate results when they want a specific style.

HOW TO PICK A NICHE FOR YOUR SHARPENING BUSINESS

You now have a better idea about the types of niches you can target when starting a sharpening business. You should also know by now just how important choosing a niche is, and that simply saying you're launching your own sharpening business is not enough. You need to niche down and be specific, as that's going to pay off not only right now, but also in the long run.

WHILE WE'VE TAKEN A CLOSER look at these factors, there is still one important thing that we should take into consideration. That is the method to follow if you want to pick a niche. There are a couple of things that you can take into consideration to help you pick a good niche. However, you also have to keep in mind that the niche you choose will impact things like who you're going to target and the level of competition you should expect.

THE FIRST QUESTION TO ask yourself is what skills you have. This is actually going to play a major role in helping you decide on the type of sharpening business you should start. If you have experience dealing with other businesses, for example, you could decide to use this to your advantage. This way, you can now go for a

B2B sharpening business niche and promote your services to restaurants, hairdressers, and even butcheries in your local area.

THERE ARE two other factors that you can use to help you pick the right niche. First, consider who you want to target. As with the example I just discussed, if you feel comfortable working with other businesses, then restaurants or perhaps hairdressers might be the ideal target market. However, that's not going to work for every person. Some would rather prefer working with individuals, such as regular residential customers, who need to get their kitchen knives sharpened. By narrowing down to the target audience you want to focus on when you start your sharpening business, it really becomes much easier to know the niche that you should focus on.

APART FROM THIS, you should also consider the goals that you have in mind for your business. Sure, you haven't really started with your business plan just yet, but it's important to already think about the long term. What do you want to achieve in, let's say, the next six months, or perhaps where do you see your business in two years from now. When you lay down a set of goals that you want to strive toward, then you can use this data to help you make a decision in terms of the niche that you should target.

SUMMARY / *Key Takeaways*

- A sharpening business is a broad term, and there are different niches within this industry. You have to narrow down and pick a niche that will work for you.
- Some examples of niches include focusing on residential knives, industrial blades, or providing your services to other businesses in your area.

- You can take things like your personal interest, experience, and expertise into consideration if you need some help deciding on which niche to target.

You now have a better idea about how you can go about picking a niche for your sharpening business. In the next section, we're going to expand more on the entire process and take a look at how you can establish a set of services that you can offer your customers.

CHAPTER 5

DECIDE WHICH SERVICES TO OFFER

N ow that you know what niche you're going to focus on and target with your sharpening business, it's time to move on to step two. In this chapter, we turn our attention to services. Now, similar to niches, you may think that you're going to start a knife sharpening business - so that's essentially going to be the service you offer. However, you have to understand that even within the knife sharpening business model, there are still different kinds of services that you can offer your clients.

BY KNOWING about the different types of services, you're giving yourself a chance to better understand the business model. You'll also be able to sit down and actually make a list of services that you're going to focus on with your business. It's important that we add this step as early as possible into the entire step-by-step process, as both in the short and long run, it's going to make keeping things organized easier. If you spend some time setting out the specific services you'll be offering, it's also going to help you define your target audience with less struggle and give you a better view of what you should expect going forward.

WHY IT PAYS TO BE SPECIFIC WITH YOUR SERVICES

First of all, why should you specify services if you already know that you're going to be sharpening blades, such as knives or scissors, as part of your business? The truth is, not every blade is the same. With that in mind, it also means if you're going to choose to offer sharpening services for any kind of blade that the customer has, then you'll need a lot of different equipment. You also have to go through more extensive training and practice sessions, as there are differences in how these blades are sharpened, too.

It's especially important to be very specific with the services you offer when you are just getting started. That's because sharpening is a skill you need to develop and work on. If you've got yourself a sharpening stone and maybe a strop, then you've been practicing on a couple of standard kitchen knives, most likely. While a sharpening stone is very useful, it's not the most ideal tool choice when you need to sharpen other blades, like axe heads and scissors.

So, in this case, you've built up experience using the sharpening stone with kitchen knives. Thus, when you become specific related to your services, you can specify "knife sharpening service", for example.

Now, you don't have to limit yourself to just a single service. You could even divide knife sharpening into multiple categories. Additionally, consider whether or not you have a strop or other polishing tools. If you do, then take advantage of these to offer an additional polishing service. This can add a niche shine to the knife and make it seem like a new one without the big investment from the customer's side.

ANOTHER REASON why you have to go through some steps to ensure you can list down services is to help you stay focused. If you don't have this kind of list, you may find yourself all over the place. You could also find yourself in a situation where you accept a job from a client, but you don't have the right equipment or the appropriate knowledge to help them. You could then hurt your reputation by offering poor service quality to that client - who can go on to tell other people about their experience. This is a type of situation that you can effectively avoid by just making sure you know what services you offer and following this list.

DIFFERENT TYPES OF SERVICES YOU CAN OFFER

You now have a better idea about why it's important to list the specific services you're going to offer. However, once you sit down with a piece of paper in front of you, you might find yourself confused about what to write down. That's why we're going to take a closer look at a couple of specific services that you could consider.

IT'S a good idea to start by considering the tools you have access to. That's going to help you understand the type of services you'll be able to offer. At first, you might only have a sharpening stone. In this case, the services you offer will likely include things like "knife sharpening by hand". Don't worry if you have limited resources, as there are some people who actually look for services that are done by hand. That's because you have a greater level of control over the angle, bevel, and the entire sharpening process when you decide to use a sharpening stone. Thus, if you're skilled, you can give people incredible results with hand sharpening. Some would even prefer hand sharpening over the use of machines on their blades.

OF COURSE, as you expand, you might want to get some machines into your workspace to speed up the flow. At that time, you could still offer hand sharpening services, alongside machine sharpening. This will add diversity and allow your customers to choose how they want their items to be sharpened.

WHEN IT COMES to picking out the services you're going to offer, you can also decide to target specific types of blades. Even within the knives sub-niche, there are still ways to be more specific. For example, you could decide to only focus on specialized tools, or perhaps solely provide sharpening services for serrated knives. This would make your business much more targeted, and you'll have an easier time getting specific in terms of the target audience you need to focus on.

APART FROM THIS, there are other ways to also expand on what you're able to offer your customers. Even if you're going to keep things simple at the beginning, you can still list some services as part of the longer-term goals that you would like to implement. Your focus will remain on blade sharpening, but adding some extra services can help to expand the audience you can target with your marketing campaigns. Plus, this can add extra income sources that you can utilize.

KNIFE REPAIR IS a good extra service that you can consider. You will need some skills for this, but it's usually easy to acquire. In fact, you can even go onto YouTube to learn some basic skills that will help you fix common issues that people run into with knives. This may include fixing a handle that broke off, for example. When you train yourself in this regard, you'll know when a knife is repairable and when it is broken to the point where it's better to get a replacement. You can then offer this kind of advice to your customers, and accept knives that can be repaired.

THIS IS ALSO where an opportunity for an extra service comes into the picture - knife sales. If you're offering services to sharpen knives, why not partner with a reputable brand and offer to sell their knives? There are some companies that accept reps in the field. In this case, you may earn a commission on every sale you are able to secure for the company. Alternatively, look into wholesale options, where you can buy knives and sets at low rates and then resell them to your customers for a profit.

THERE ARE different scenarios where this can be useful. For example, when someone comes to you for knife repair, but you notice that the knife cannot be repaired due to the way it's broken, you have an opportunity to promote a new set of knives to that person. It's a great way to make sure you don't have to turn customers away when you're unable to help them. You can still use this type of situation as an opportunity to secure a sale and grow your business.

WHILE WE'RE on the subject of selling items, consider offering your customers a few items that they can use to keep their knives sharp at home. Of course, you don't want to create competition for yourself, so this will generally not include the sale of actual sharpening stones. Instead, you could stock a few simple sharpening tools that help with maintenance. You can then instruct the customer on how the tool works and give them details about how frequently they should use the item. They will still rely on you for a more thorough sharpening service, and have these items to keep the knife sharp after you sharpened their blades.

Now, with all of this said, it's still important to make sure you keep in mind your target audience, what you have access to, and the local community. Some services will do better with specific types of target audiences. That means you have to take into consideration the niche that you've selected, for example.

HOW TO CHOOSE THE RIGHT SERVICES FOR YOUR BUSINESS

You should now have a better idea about how targeting specific services works. We also went over the specific types of services that you could consider. This may include more than just knife sharpening solutions, such as knife sales, repairs, and more. Now, at this point, it's time to begin listing down those services that you are going to focus on.

You can take a closer look at a couple of things to make the process easier. Once again, your target audience comes into play here. You need to know who you want to offer your services to. When you have a better idea about your market, then you can start to determine the type of services that they will likely be interested in. It starts with the sharpening services, of course, but consider if there are any specific types of blades that they tend to use. This will also help you understand if extra services, such as repairs and sales, could be a good fit.

· · ·

THE GOALS that you have in mind for your business also come into play here. You have to consider where you want to see your business headed in the future - and that means both short and long term goals. The services you choose to offer should properly align with where you want to take your business.

SUMMARY / *Key Takeaways*

- Choosing what services you're going to offer your customers is important. You should do this before you get into the technical aspects of setting up your business plan and deciding how you're going to market your services to potential customers.
- It's important to keep a few things in mind when you choose what services to offer. This includes your target audience, the goals you want to set for your business, and what specific equipment and tools you have at your disposal.

IN THE NEXT CHAPTER, we're going to turn our focus to pricing. The thing about a sharpening business is, as you've seen already, that you have to start thinking about services and several other factors at an early stage. Setting the pricing once you know what services you're going to offer plays an important role in making things feel more organized and professional. It's also going to ease the process of giving out quotes and sending invoices once you start to offer your services to customers.

CHAPTER 6

SET YOUR PRICES

P ricing your knife sharpening services can be a tricky task. But if you want to be successful, you need to find a balance between being competitive and making a profit. This chapter provides detailed guidelines on how to set prices for your knife sharpening business. Including some tips and tricks on picking out different pricing models.

HOW PRICING AFFECTS YOUR BUSINESS

Pricing is the backbone of your business strategy. Choosing a price that is too high or too low can have negative effects on your business. If the price is too high, it might deter customers. But, if it is too low, you may not be able to sustain your business or cover the expenses.

A WELL-DESIGNED pricing strategy can affect how successful your company is in three ways: how much money it makes (profit), how customers behave when it comes to your business (consumer behavior), and their general impression of your knife sharpening services (brand image).

FOR YOUR BUSINESS TO SUCCEED, you need to maintain cash flow. An excellent pricing plan is twice as effective as boosting retention and four times more efficient than improving an acquisition. This means that setting the right prices can be much more effective for business growth compared to just trying to hold on to current customers or trying to get new ones.

The other aspect is not price. It's value. You need to understand the differences between cost, prices, and value.

- The cost of your knife sharpening service is the amount you spend to make it. It encompasses the expenses related to the materials, labor, and equipment you are using in the sharpening process.
- The price you set is the fee that the customer pays for the quality and expertise you provide. It is the financial reward for your time and skills.
- But, the true measure of success lies in the perceived value your customers have for the service. The value is what your customer believes that the knife sharpening service is worth to them.

YOUR KNIFE SHARPENING business must cover the costs to make a profit. Divide the costs into two elements: fixed costs and variable costs.

FIXED costs stay the same regardless of how many customers you have. These are salaries, rent, business rates, etc. Variable costs go up as you sell more. Such as labor, materials, and transport.

- When you decide on a price, make sure it is higher than the variable cost. This way, each sale helps cover the expenses and helps you pay off the fixed costs, leaving you with a better profit.

TO MAXIMIZE YOUR EARNINGS, set prices that reflect the value you provide. Know the factors that influence your customer's buying habits, like how convenient your service is, how reliable it is, and how quickly it is delivered. Understand the advantages your customers get from using your service. But, this can be unique to every customer.

FOR EXAMPLE, some customers want tools that last. So, they are willing to pay more. Others need a convenient cooking experience - the cheaper the better.

UNDERSTANDING your target audience can help you define a market of potential customers who want to purchase your services and can afford them. This decreases the risk of wasted marketing expenses on trying to attract the wrong target audience.

- Pricing on its own will not dictate the profitability of your business. Another important factor is price over quantity and over time.

LET's say you are offering knife sharpening at a 10 times higher rate than your costs. But, if you only service one knife per day, you won't be able to sustain your business. Even though the fee for your service is high, you won't be able to cover the expenses.

THAT's because it is not just about the price, but finding the right balance between volume and pricing over time. To put it in perspective, you need to make a decent profit with a consistent flow of customers, ideally a couple a day.

ANOTHER IMPORTANT FACTOR when setting your price is speed and efficiency. Think about the speed at which you can sharpen knives and how many customers you can serve in a day. A more efficient process allows for a higher volume and better profit margin.

IDEALLY, your prices should align with the prices of your competitors. If the prices are too low, your customers will think that your brand is too "cheap" and not good enough. It will also be very difficult to make a profit.

BUT, if the prices are too high, then you risk losing potential customers to your competition. That's because customers will get the impression that you are a "luxury" brand, which is something not everyone can afford.

OVERALL, it is important that you are able to convince customers that parting with a couple of bucks is better than using dull knives.

METHODS FOR SETTING PRICES

There are different ways you can use to set prices for your services. You could charge by the hour, by the job, or by the blade.

WITH AN HOURLY RATE, you charge customers based on the amount of time it takes to sharpen their knives. This method provides a straightforward and transparent way to charge for your time and expertise. It can also be flexible if some knives require more time than others. But, customers who need many knives sharpened, are less likely to prefer to pay an hourly rate.

IF YOU SET the price by the job, you set a standard fee for sharpening a specific number of knives, regardless of the time it takes. This gives customers a clear and predictable cost for the service, which is more appealing and convenient for those who need more knives sharpened. But, you need to carefully estimate the time and effort it takes for every job to get done.

HOWEVER, if you decide to charge by the blade, then you get more flexibility for billing. Every sharpened knife has a different cost. But, some knives might require more work than others, so you will need to consider a fair average price per blade.

THE PRICE per knife is often the same. It can range from $1 to $2 per inch of the blade or every knife. This cost can vary based on the type of knife you are working on. Yet, this is the most common flat rate.

But, if your customer is in need of more services other than just a sharpening job, then they can pay additional fees. For a bent knife, you can add anywhere from $5 to $10 to the bill. Fixing broken blade tips and knives can cost somewhere from $5 to $20.

For chipped edges in need of repair, you are looking at an extra $5 to $20, based on the type of knife you are working with. Thinning the blade is another add-on, which could cost about $10. Since it increases the blade's performance and strength, it guarantees high-quality results.

Let's break it down with a relatable example. You need to work on a standard chef's knife, about 8 inches long, only in need of sharpening. Let's assign a base cost of 1.00 to this service. Using the same pricing system, we'd also calculate the cost of sharpening other items.

Take, for instance, a 4-inch paring knife. Besides this entry, you'd indicate the percentage of the cost in comparison to the original chef's knife. If sharpening the chef's knife costs 4 units of the local currency and sharpening the paring knife costs 3 units, it would look like this: 8 inches chef's knife - 1.00 and 4 inches paring knife - 0.75.

You would extend this list to cover all the various knives and tools you plan to sharpen. You can also include any additional services, like repairing broken knife points, and relate their costs as a percentage of the chef's knife sharpening fee.

REMEMBER, the specific currency isn't crucial here. What matters is understanding how the costs of other services compare to the cost of sharpening the chef's knife.

YOU ALSO NEED to know what people are paying in your local area to have their chef's knife sharpened. So, visit your local stores or browse their services online to get a better perspective. This way, you should get close to the ideal price range.

FOR RETURNING CUSTOMERS, you can also offer discounts for multiple blades. If you open a contract with another business, you can also set up a subscription-based service, where clients pay a monthly fee to get a certain number of sharpenings.

SOME OF THE businesses that can highly benefit from your knife sharpening services are machine shops, restaurants, sheep shearers, farms, hair salons, cheese shops, fishing boats, wood shops, and more. So, advertise your services in your local area to build a steady business client base.

CHOOSING THE RIGHT PRICING MODEL FOR YOUR BUSINESS

Your prices must remain market-relevant. The pricing model you go for will vary based on many factors. Such as your target market, business goals, and the type of services you provide.

. . .

THIS WAY, customers are more likely to buy your service and less likely to turn to your competition. There are different ways to achieve that with some of the following pricing strategies.

PENETRATION PRICING IS a popular strategy for a start-up business. When you use low-entry pricing, you are offering your services at lower costs to draw in customers. You can do this when you are introducing your business into the market. But, this is not a sustainable pricing strategy. To gain a competitive advantage you would need to gradually increase the prices to obtain a higher profit margin. With enough value and a great service, you can start scaling your business.

FOR EXAMPLE, you can use penetration pricing if you are targeting more budget-conscious consumers. Charging by the blade is the cheapest pricing option and a relatively popular choice for customers who want to save money.

ANOTHER OPTION IS PROMOTIONAL PRICING. Offering special limited-time discounts can help double your sales. This is a great pricing strategy for boosting sales volume during the holidays or special events. But, keep in mind that even though you are selling more, the overall profit earned from each sale may be less compared to selling the service at full price.

CAPTIVE PRICING IS ALSO POPULAR. It means providing combo deals to attract more customers to your business. This tactic involves packaging some extra items with your service and selling them as a bundle. This can be an excellent tactic if you are working with other businesses, like restaurants or hair salons.

· · ·

IF YOUR SERVICES are more expensive, but you need to work on your customer retention, then you can attract more customers by including a couple of freebies or non-monetary incentives. For example, provide your customers a free knife sharpening with every 10 purchases, or a free knife block.

BUT, if you are selling custom knives or other products that can be displayed on the shelves, then you can use psychological pricing. This type of pricing strategy targets human psychology to improve sales.

FOR EXAMPLE, you can use the "9-digit" effect. You can write a price tag of $499 for a custom knife that's worth $500. Another method is to put a more expensive knife next to that cheaper custom knife. Or, you could offer the customer to buy one custom knife and get 50% off on the next one. Deals such as these are too good and hard to pass up.

SUMMARY / *Key Takeaways*

- Every knife-sharpening business needs to find a proper balance between staying ahead of the game and making a profit.
- Remember, it is difficult to penetrate the market as a new business owner. But, if you research the competition and your target audience, you can set yourself up for success.
- There are different ways you can start setting your prices. You can charge by the hour, by the job, or by the blade.
- Your pricing strategy should align with your business goals. Whether you choose to use methods like

competitive pricing or penetration pricing, you must make sure your business can cover your expenses and remain popular among customers.

- Consider providing added value or incentives to improve customer satisfaction and loyalty.

IN THE NEXT CHAPTER, we'll go over setting up your own dedicated space for sharpening.

CHAPTER 7
CREATE YOUR WORKSPACE

O nce you create your prices and define the services that your knife-sharpening business is going to provide, it's time to focus on creating your workspace. Your workspace is just as important as your sharpening skills when you're starting your business. The work environment is where you're going to spend most of your time during the day. You want to make it practical and easy to navigate, but at the same time, your work environment should complement your personality and send a positive message to your clients.

THE WHOLE PROCESS of starting any kind of business can be overwhelming. This chapter has got you covered! The following pages will take you through everything you need to know about setting up a work environment, equipment and supplies, and business tools you are going to need.

WHERE TO SET UP YOUR WORKSPACE

One of the first decisions you'll need to make when starting a knife sharpening business is where to set up your work environment. Let's describe this decision as the foundation on which you're going to build your business. You have two main options to consider. One option is to set up workspace at home. The second option is to rent a dedicated space. Both options have pros and cons.

WHICH ONE TO CHOOSE, you're probably wondering. The most practical approach is to compare both options i.e. their advantages and disadvantages to see which type of workspace suits you the most.

PROS OF SETTING up a workspace at your home include:

- **Lower overhead costs:** you can significantly lower your expenses by operating from home. Doing so eliminates the costs of renting a space, utilities, and other expenses that business owners have with a separate location.
- **More flexibility:** setting up a workspace at home gives you more flexibility in terms of working hours, you can adapt them however it feels convenient to you.
- **No commute:** a major advantage of setting up a workspace at home is that you can avoid the stress associated with daily commutes to and from work.

CONS OF SETTING workspace at your home include:

- **Lack of privacy** (if you're sharing living space with others)
- **Safety concerns** (if children are around)

ON THE OTHER HAND, the pros of renting a space include:

- **Professional storefront:** a rented space gives your business a proper storefront where you can interact with customers. Plus, it improves your credibility.
- **Better work-life balance:** by keeping working and living areas separate, you get to improve productivity and quality of life.
- **No disruptions:** In a rented space, you can focus only on the task at hand and nothing else. You won't have to worry about noise, mess, or anyone coming across sharp objects.

CONS OF RENTING A SPACE INCLUDE:

- **Higher expenses** due to rent, which could affect your profit
- **Limited flexibility** in terms of working hours

LIKE IN REAL ESTATE, setting up a workspace is all about location. There are no "one size fits all" rules here. You have the freedom to choose an option that suits your needs and preferences the most. Compare the pros and cons of both options. Choose the option whose advantages outweigh the disadvantages.

FOR EXAMPLE, a person who prefers flexibility in working hours and wants to avoid expenses associated with rent could benefit from setting up a workspace at home. Of course, this depends on whether they have enough space for their equipment. On the flip side, a person who doesn't like to mix private and professional life will opt for renting a space. The most important thing to know is that there is no right or wrong answer.

REGARDLESS OF THE option you choose, make sure the working environment has good lighting and ventilation and that it can accommodate your equipment.

TOOLS OF THE TRADE

Now that you made a decision regarding the location of your workspace, it's time to focus on the tools you're going to need. You need two types of tools: sharpening tools and business tools. You can easily consider those tools the essentials i.e. items and pieces of equipment that are necessary to operate a knife sharpening business. Choosing tools and equipment depends on the type of sharpening operations you plan to perform. Don't worry; it's a lot easier than you think.

Sharpening tools

Since you're planning to start a knife sharpening business, you already have some tools in mind. Some of them have been mentioned in the previous chapter as well. Below you can see what equipment and sharpening tools you're going to need to ensure your knife sharpening business runs smoothly.

SHARPENING stones

A couple of sets of sharpening stones are necessary to restore the edge of a blade. Different grit levels correspond to different levels of sharpening. You may want to invest in a variety of sharpening stones to ensure smooth operation. For instance, dealing with rough sharpening where you need to remove chips along the edge or to restore dull blades calls for sharpening stones from 120 to 400 grit. Normal sharpening generally requires sharpening stones from 700 to 1200-2000 grit. For polishing the surface and removing find scratches, you may need a sharpening stone with 2000 grit. When it comes to finishing sharpening stones, 8000 grit is a good choice or anything between 3000 and 6000 grit.

IT'S ALSO useful to get sharpening stones in different sizes. As an owner of a knife-sharpening business, you want to have the perfect sharpening stone for every knife to ensure customer satisfaction. Plus, sharpening is a lot more effective when you match the size of the blade to the size of the stone. Choose the size of a sharpening stone that allows you to sweep in one motion the entire length of the blade across the stone.

SHARPENING guide

If you're new to the world of professional knife sharpening, you need a sharpening guide to maintain a consistent angle while sharpening. A sharpening guide is a tool that clips on the back of a knife so you can sharpen it like a pro. This is the best way to ensure a uniform edge. The sharpening guide also provides stability, which is important when you're developing your skills and trying to get more experience.

TRANSPORTATION

If you plan to make your knife sharpening business mobile, you need a rolling suitcase or a toolbox to transport your equipment from one place to another. That way, your sharpening stones and other tools are stored properly and easy to reach when you need them. Everything you need is available in a toolbox or a rolling suitcase.

WHEN IT COMES TO TRANSPORTATION, you also need a mode of transportation. This depends entirely on you and your equipment. In most cases, a van is sufficient.

You may want to consider making your knife-sharpening business mobile, as many entrepreneurs do. Customers may find it convenient, and it's also a good marketing move for your business.

Some knife-sharpening business owners make their entire business mobile to reduce overhead costs.

MACHINERY

For advanced sharpening operations, you may want to consider smaller and more affordable machines that can speed up the sharpening process. At the beginning, when you're starting your business and working on your experience, it's wiser to start smaller and work your way to pricier and more elaborate pieces of equipment.

WHEN YOU'RE CREATING an efficient workspace and choosing the tools, you should take several factors into consideration. For example, you may want to invest in a quality workbench that is both comfortable and ergonomically designed. You also need proper lighting, good ventilation, and implement safety measures. Keep your workspace organized to maximize your efficiency.

Business tools

Starting any kind of business calls for the use of a wide spectrum of tools associated with customer service, marketing, and payment processing. The main purpose of business tools is to increase efficiency and save time. They're necessary for the smooth functioning of your knife-sharpening business. So, the business tools you're going to need are described below.

MARKETING MATERIALS

As a business owner, you need a well-structured marketing strategy to promote your business and attract customers. One of the easiest ways to make it happen is through simple marketing materials such as brochures, business cards, and flyers. They should contain your contact information and describe the services you provide.

SOFTWARE FOR INVOICES and estimates of costs

The more professional tools you use, the higher your credibility. Professional software for invoices and cost estimates ensures accuracy and also saves time. You don't have to struggle creating invoices when you can just use software and have it completed in a matter of minutes. Everything that maximizes efficiency is a good addition to your knife-sharpening business.

CUSTOMER MANAGEMENT SOFTWARE

Even a regular paper calendar will do, but it's a lot more efficient to use customer management software, computer calendar, or Google calendar to set up reminders for appointments. Doing so allows you to keep track of your customers. Plus, you won't forget anything. After all, despite maximum efforts, it's easy to forget appointments. This is especially the case in times of stress. With software or a calendar, you will avoid this problem.

PAYMENT PROCESSING **tool**

Set up a payment processing system that will allow you to accept payments from your customers. You may want to consider credit card processing and other digital payment methods. These tools offer full transparency. However, if you plan to make your knife sharpening business cash-only, then you need a safe to store your money in the safest way possible.

WEBSITE DEVELOPMENT

In the digital area, where people spend most of their time online, it's useful to have a website that provides detailed insight into your knife sharpening business. Developing a website is an investment, especially when it's mobile-friendly, but it can benefit you in the long run. You don't need an elaborate website unless you want to, but a simple site could be of huge help in promoting your services. The website is like an ID card of your business in a way that it displays all the most relevant information. You can present your services and show off your expertise by setting up a blog section. In other words, a website is a powerful tool for business owners.

ONLINE PRESENCE

Not all tools for your knife sharpening business are physical. Online presence can also be considered a tool that helps you take your digital marketing strategy to a new level. If you plan to create content to promote your business, you will need to invest in a good phone and other pieces of equipment, such as a tripod.

Creating content is also a powerful tool that you can use to run your knife-sharpening business and promote it to a larger group of people. Social media allows you to build trust and credibility with your audience. By sharing content that relates to knife-sharpening, you get to establish your reputation as an expert in this field. This leads to more customers and bigger profits.

KEEP in mind that it's not mandatory to use the abovementioned tools. The equipment and tools you use depend on your needs and preferences or how you want to run your knife sharpening business. Compared to some other types of small businesses, knife-sharpening business doesn't require a fortune to get started. Even if you're on a limited budget, you can still get everything you need.

SUMMARY / *Key Takeaways*

- Your workspace is equally important as your skills
- Sharpening stone, sharpening guide, and simple machinery are all you need when starting your knife sharpening business
- Consider implementing software and other useful tools to maximize your efficiency

THIS CHAPTER TOOK you through the process of setting up your workspace. As you can see, it's a lot easier than you think. Always consider your needs and preferences when making choices regarding location and equipment. Once you set up your workspace, it's time to work and interact with customers. Chapter 8 explains how to develop a process for sharpening knives and interacting with customers.

CHAPTER 8

FIGURE OUT YOUR PROCESS

A well-oiled machine runs smoothly and efficiently. The same can be said for your knife sharpening business process. Many start-ups fail because they lack a well-planned business process, or their existing one doesn't align with the overall vision of that business. Things are happening all over the place. Nobody knows where anything is, how many orders they got, or what stage is the sharpening process. When you step into a company that doesn't have a figured-out process, you can immediately see why it is not reaching its full potential.

Here, you can learn how to develop a process for your sharpening business, from simplifying operations and reducing risks to improving customer satisfaction.

THE IMPORTANCE OF HAVING A PROCESS

Your process is what turns a one-time customer into a lifelong client. It is what takes a messy, dull knife, and transforms it into a thing of beauty. But, most importantly, your business process helps topple your competition.

A survey by Work Insight Reports shows that 70% of business leaders spend more than 40% of their core time on mundane tasks. Meanwhile, 71% of workers are wasting nearly 20% of their work time in a similar manner. Over 50% of companies are actively working to enhance their business process because they understand that a business thrives when its processes are in sync with the overall goals of the organization. Efficient business process is the bedrock of your business. It is what gives your company organization, structure, and support. A process is a chain of procedures, actions, and steps assigned to specific team members to provide the necessary outcomes to the client.

There are various types of processes. Such as primary, support, and management business processes. Primary processes are the essential operations in a business where the final product or service is handed over directly to the customer. Every action and quality check in these processes aims to add value to your knife sharpening service.Support processes may not directly affect the value of your service, but they play a crucial role in ensuring that the primary processes run without a hitch. These processes support the day-to-day functioning of your business. Management processes help you oversee how your business operates. These processes allow you to establish objectives and guidelines that are important for both primary and support processes. This category covers different levels of planning - from long-term strategies to immediate actions. It also involves supervision and regulation of various aspects of your business.

For a company to reach a tangible goal, each team member must carry out their duties accordingly, even if it means repeating certain steps many times. This helps employees stay on task.

An effective business process not only helps you spot inefficiencies before they get out of hand, but it also allows you to achieve reliable outcomes and scale your business.

Knowing your process helps your start-up be more efficient and spend less valuable time on tasks that are not important.

With a process, you can collaborate better with your employees and spend less time coordinating via chat or email.

If you don't see the worth of improving your process and you are satisfied with the status quo, you can't keep up with your competitors.

The process lays out the most effective approach to completing a task and considers the potential challenges. Tasks are given to employees who have the skills and knowledge to get the job done, therefore decreasing the risk of error.

With a solid process, the adequate moves and steps are clearly mapped out. This improves worker productivity and task efficiency.

A business process keeps your company in the loop about what customers want and their opinions on the service or product they get. By using market research and feedback, you can communicate with customers more effectively.

When there is no standardized process, it increases the risk of mistakes, which ends up costing the business time, money, and resources. There are long wait times, delays, and a backlog of work. This leads to dissatisfied customers and puts a strain on your staff.

If you are starting a small business or a home office, you won't need too many employees. But, as you get more customers, you will need staff who will fill those roles.

To get more customer orders done and provide faster services, you need knife sharpeners who are familiar with the trade. For accounting and scheduling your appointments, a general manager can provide the necessary services.

But, if you are planning to grow your business and reach a wide range of clients, then you would need to invest in a marketing team, such as a social media specialist or SEO strategist. When you are planning your business process, you need to think about the tasks of each individual in your team.

BREAKING DOWN THE STEPS OF YOUR BUSINESS

There are a couple of things you need to consider when developing your process.

First, you need to decide what kind of knives/blades you are going to sharpen. You should be able to sharpen any knife, like a pocket knife, serrated, streak, kitchen knife, hunting knife, and scissors.

But, each type has unique features and requirements for sharpening. For example, to sharpen a serrated knife, you would need to sharpen the flat side, not the serrated side. Most of the work requires a process known as deburring, not sharpening or grinding.

If you decide to sharpen a diverse range of knives, it means you'll need to have a versatile setup. This can impact factors like the total time spent on each sharpening session and the logistical arrangements for handling various types of blades.

The time required for each sharpening session varies based on the type of blade you are working with. For example, specialized and larger blades often need more time and attention compared to standard kitchen knives.

It's critical to allocate enough time for different processes, especially when you are working with a variety of blades. This ensures that you deliver quality service without rushing the process.

Different types of blades may come with an additional set of logistical challenges. For example, larger blades require more workspace and a sturdier setup. Specialized blades need specific tools or fixtures for optimal sharpening.

If you plan to sharpen larger blades or multiple knives at once, you'll need a bigger workspace. For projects such as these, you would also need a bigger team. Or, if you plan on taking the jobs yourself, you need to plan your time accordingly.

Get a diverse set of sharpening stones, honing rods, and

other equipment tailored to the variety of blades you will work with. Keep them organized and within reach.

If you prefer to use a power grinder, then nothing beats the speed and simplicity of a set of paper wheels on a bench grinder. But, it is important to note that they can't handle heavy work, like fixing broken tips, reducing bolsters, or sharpening extremely dull knives.

Once you've decided on the types of knives you will sharpen and the workspace you need, it's time to determine how you will collect the knives from your clients. This is a key step in ensuring a convenient and seamless business process.

The first method is on-site pickup. By offering your clients to collect the knives from them, you provide a more appealing option for clients who value convenience. It's a service-oriented approach that can accommodate the needs of customers of all ages.

For example, imagine a busy restaurant owner who needs their kitchen knives sharpened. The owner doesn't have the time to take the knives to your business. But, when you offer to go there yourself or send one of your staff members to collect the knives directly, you help your customer save valuable time.

Another method is the drop-off. If you have a physical location where customers can drop off their knives, you can use this method to stay in touch with clients and allow them to see your workspace. This is a great option for building trust in your services.

For example, a client who is interested in having their knives sharpened, but also likes to browse your wares, would prefer to drop them off at your designated location.

The third method is a mail-based service. Customers can secure a package or a service and send their knives to you via mail. This is an excellent approach for serving clients beyond your local area.

By providing multiple collection options, you improve the accessibility of your knife sharpening services. However, this approach requires a robust system for safely receiving, processing, and returning knives via mail.

For example, you have customers who live in different cities or overseas. They will prefer to send you knives through a mail-based service. Ultimately, you can use the method to build a diverse client base and grow your business.

Now, you need to decide how you will return the knives to your customers. You need a reliable system for returning the final product. Offering a mail-based return service is a popular option for clients who want their sharpened knives to arrive at their doorstep. But, this process does require meticulous planning, packaging, labeling, and coordinating the return shipment.

Many people wonder if you sharpen a knife for a customer, how do you pack and transport it after it has been sharpened? You can put some blue painter's tape over the edge. For additional protection, professionals often use an edge protector, knife sleeves, or a blade guard. So, it is a good idea to have them at your disposal. You would then place the sharp knife in a sturdy container, such as a knife case or a knife roll. Seal and label the package since it contains sharp objects.

To prevent movement within the container, professionals in the trade often use packing material like foam, bubble wrap, or packing peanuts to fill any empty spaces. This ensures the knives stay in place during transit.

A local-only drop-off/pickup policy is a great option for customers who prefer a more personal touch. They have to physically visit your designated location to retrieve the sharpened knife. But, this process is only useful if you are serving customers in your vicinity.

The final step is to ensure a smooth and secure payment process. It's best to offer a variety of payment methods to accommodate the needs of a diverse consumer base. This can include options like cash, credit/debit, mobile payment apps, and online payment platforms.

You also need a transparent pricing structure that clearly

outlines the cost of your services. This transparency builds trust with your customers and avoids any potential misunderstandings.

Providing invoices and receipts is a standard practice. It is a formal record of the transactions that demonstrates your commitment to accountability and professionalism.

Ideally, you should use the latest technologies to enhance your business process. It's important to assess the specific needs and goals of your business. This way, you can determine which technologies would be the most useful.

For example, PRISM Visual Software can be used for inventory management, order processing, collecting payments, tracking, and managing workflow. This software technology can help reduce manual effort and increase efficiency.

Document Data Extraction can be valuable for managing customer information, order details, and invoices. Automated data extraction can save time and reduce the risk of errors that come with manual data entry.

AI-powered chatbots or virtual assistants can handle customer inquiries, provide information about services, and even assist in appointment scheduling. This improves customer engagement and helps your workers focus on priority tasks.

DEVELOPING YOUR OWN PROCESS

Once you have considered all the factors involved in knife sharpening, you can start developing your own process. Remember, there is no one-size-fits-all solution here. Your process will be unique to your sharpening business.

But, overall, try the following steps:

- **Step 1: Review your workflow** - Talk to every member of your team, or have someone communicate about their tasks, including you as the owner. Then figure out the most efficient way to handle every aspect of your business. A simple way to start would be to see how another professional sharpener does things so that you can mirror them. You can also analyze other businesses in similar industries and see how they work.

- **Step 2: Document the process:** Record the most efficient methods you've pinpointed in detail, preferably in digital format. That way you will make sure that everyone is on the same page.
- **Step 3: Ensure compliance:** Each member of the team must have the right training. They should know the business process and execute the tasks consistently. You can do regular inspections and document the progress, or have a manager who ensures compliance.
- **Step 4: Automate the process:** Identify and eliminate sources of waste in your operations. Continue to assess and update the process to make your business more efficient. Automation decreases human errors, boosts value, and improves efficiency.
- **Step 5: Create a self-reliant company:** Evaluate your operations and recognize any areas where your knife-sharpening business is overly reliant on specific people, like customers, suppliers, or staff. This overdependence can be risky because if there's a problem with any of these key players, it can disrupt the business. What you can do is gradually delegate more responsibilities to capable managers as the business grows. This shift allows the owner to focus on higher-level strategic thinking and planning for the future. So, hire people you can trust and have the experience you need.

Don't forget, the process doesn't have to be complicated. In fact, the simpler it is, the easier it is to get all the employees to work toward the same goal. With a simple process, you can give your clients sharper edges in a short amount of time and still provide quality services that keep people coming back for more.

DOCUMENTING YOUR PROCESS

As your business expands, it becomes more complicated. There are more people to train, more steps to follow, and more tasks to finish. It is difficult to organize your business process without documenting it.

Process documentation provides a detailed and clear guideline of how a business process works. This documentation covers timelines, tools, roles, outputs, inputs, and more. To do that, you can simply create a written list of steps that you and your employees should follow.

Or, you could use software that takes a more systematic approach and you can use it as you scale your operations. You can then share your documented process with your team and work together to find any problems.

First, choose a process. Decide which task you want to document. Understand why it's important for the organization. Then, you can define the scope. Describe what's part of the process and what's not.

For the documentation to be efficient, you need to set boundaries. Know where the process starts, what triggers it, and how you'll know it's done. Understand what the process will produce or achieve. Don't forget to note down the resources needed for each step.

Next, get input from those who know the process well. You can do that by inspiring the team to brainstorm the process steps. List the steps from start to finish, put them in a clear order, and use your team's insight to get creative.

After listing the steps, it's time to decide who will be responsible for each step. To keep things professional, many business owners are using job titles instead of names.

To improve the documentation process, try to use visuals. Options like a flowchart can help your team visualize the steps, which is a lot easier for keeping track of different tasks. You can also use graphics, examples, screenshots, color coding, etc.

If you have a larger team, consider exceptions. Sometimes, the process might change, for example, more workers may be sick and can't finish their tasks on time. You need to note any exceptions and list ways on how to handle them.

By measuring the process's success rate, you can improve and control your business. Go over the process with everyone involved and test it a couple of times to see if there are any potential issues you would like to change.

To develop the best documentation practices, try to keep the documents simple and on-point. It should be straightforward and provide accurate information, but in a way that is easy for the reader to understand.

Don't use too many charts and complex documents with unnecessary details, as your team can get confused. Basically, you need to strike a balance between accuracy and simplicity for effective communication.

Establish a clear strategy for updating your documents, in case the process changes. Also, it is best to go through these documents, at least once a year to make sure the process is up to date. Or, you could assign someone from your team to regularly review, update the document, and notify the team.

For every business process, you need to have separate documentation. This helps avoid confusion. Store the documents for easy access and have them distributed to everyone. You can store the documents online.

A digital method of your business process helps you make regular updates. You can use free apps, such as Google Docs, or opt for business management software that provides functionalities like notifications, workflow planning, and dashboards.

But, if you are not using a standard template, then you can create a documentation guide. This can be used to introduce every new member of your team to the documented material. With a bit of effort, you can create quality documents that can benefit your business in the long run.

Summary / *Key Takeaways*

- You need a business process to make your sharpening business stand out and make a mark in a crowded market.
- There are a couple of things to consider when figuring out your process. That includes the type of blades you will sharpen and how to collect and distribute them to your customers.
- Start developing your own process and get creative. Bear in mind that your process will be one-of-a-kind and tailored to your business.

In the next chapter, we'll talk about how to get your first paying customers.

CHAPTER 9
FIND CUSTOMERS

A knife sharpening business is nothing without customers. But, the key to success is the quality of the services you provide as well as the personality you present to your customers. Without either of those things, you can't get a loyal customer base.

BY FINDING the right advertising efforts, you can put your business on the map. Here is how to find clients and stimulate customer retention.

THE IMPORTANCE OF MARKETING

As a startup, your main goal is to generate interest and awareness in your knife-sharpening services. People can't know what you offer unless you put your name out there.

MARKETING IS PARTICULARLY important because it helps your business disrupt current industries and introduce your services.

77

It allows you to build your brand identity, capture the attention of potential clients, and differentiate yourself from your competition.

ANOTHER CRUCIAL COMPONENT of marketing is customer acquisition. Your knife sharpening business should attract and convert new clients quickly to get more profit and expand the business. This means combining different marketing tactics that resonate with your client base.

HERE IS a list of marketing strategies that work for a knife-sharpening business.

PRINT ADVERTISING

In standard marketing, flyers are an organic way to reach customers. They are a cheap and effective method for building brand awareness. Even if people don't actually convert into a client, they still see your brand and the services you provide.

YOU CAN DESIGN precise and detailed flyers exactly as you want them. But, without effective design and layout, these flyers will most likely end up in the trash.

TO CREATE SUCCESSFUL PRINT ADVERTISING, don't cram your flyer with too much information. Sometimes, less is more, and using white space can be a powerful attention-grabber.

The design should be minimal. People don't have to put in the effort to search for information or take too much time to read. Everything about your knife sharpening business is visible on the first or second page.

. . .

HAND YOUR CUSTOMERS what they want to see. Determine your main message or call to action, and put it on the first page. If you are promoting a sale or a discount, make that message stand out.

USE CATCHY AND INTERESTING DESIGNS, vibrant colors, and bold fonts to highlight the value of your offer. Include bullet points, high-resolution images, and the company logo.

To distribute the flyers, you can send them via mail, hand them out at events or public spaces, personally deliver them door-to-door, pin them up on notice boards, or set up flyer holders in places your potential clients frequent.

LOCAL FARMERS MARKET

To connect with the local community, get a booth at your local farmer's market and sharpen knives and tools on-site.

FARMERS' Markets are a highly popular method of direct marketing. These markets attract a diverse crowd, including chefs, gardeners, and farmers, who are more likely to be interested in your sharpening services. This gives you direct access to your target audience.

THIS OPPORTUNITY HELPS your business establish a physical presence in the community and enhances your brand's recognition among the local residents. Since you will be demonstrating your knife sharpening skills on the spot, customers can see your services firsthand.

. . .

To be successful at a farmer's market, you need to build the business through promotion and networking. When people first see you at the booth, they will ask if you will be here next week. So, you should have a regular presence, like every week or every other week.

Another major benefit comes from collaborations and partnerships. Having a knife sharpener around attracts customers to the farmer's market. People tend to browse and shop for about an hour while their knives are getting sharpened. Once the market realizes the extra attention you bring, they may want to feature you in their promotions. When the markets advertise your skills in the newspaper, you can get a surge of clients.

However, sharpening knives at a farmer's market may not provide a full-time income. Mainly due to the market's seasonal nature. But, it is a great option for connecting with people and showing off your skills in real-time.

COMMUNITY FORUMS

Community forums are online platforms where people with shared goals and interests collaborate and interact on different topics. These are platforms you can use for self-promotion.

People, organizations, and businesses often set up and manage community forums for their clients to connect, ask for advice, or find new ideas. You can use these forums as a tool to find customers.

. . .

THERE ARE knife sharpener forums where users ask questions, offer tips, and work together to solve different projects. When you actively participate in these forums, you establish yourself as a knowledgeable and trustworthy expert in knife sharpening.

YOU PROVIDE VALUABLE INSIGHT, which can build your credibility. For example, you can have threads or sections dedicated to knife maintenance or other related topics that can showcase your expertise.

FORUMS CAN ALSO BE useful when you want to announce promotions, discounts, or any other events related to your business. Feel free to engage the community by building a positive presence. Positive feedback can help attract more clients, while constructive criticism can help improve your services.

TEAM UP WITH LOCAL BUSINESSES

Collaboration with local businesses provides a mutual benefit. Collaborations provide a steady customer base and expand your presence within the community. However, this marketing strategy requires a proactive approach.

YOU CAN PARTNER up at industry trade shows, or use online directories like Google My Business, Yelp, or Yellow Pages to find local butcher shops, pet groomers, cafes, restaurants, or other food-related businesses. Reach out to them and propose a partnership.

YOU CAN USE social media platforms like LinkedIn to search for and connect with owners or managers. If you prefer to showcase your expertise and expand your reach, you can host workshops or demonstrations of knife sharpening and maintenance. Then invite local businesses and people in your vicinity to attend.

GO MOBILE

If you can't afford a permanent shop and want lower overhead costs, then you can try mobile marketing. By leveraging the mobility of a small enclosed trailer, truck, or van, you can take your advertisement directly to your target audience and maximize engagement and exposure.

THESE MOBILE BILLBOARDS target specific demographics and geographical areas, usually within a local community. They provide flexibility and convenience, allowing you to adapt to different markets, events, or areas.

TO FIND CUSTOMERS, you need to transform your mobile billboard with an impressive design. Invest in creative advertisements that stand out in an urban landscape. These advertisements should be visible even when the truck or trailer is not in use.

Compared to print or TV media, putting your advertisements on trailers and trucks is a more budget-friendly approach. It's like hitting a bullseye with your marketing efforts since you will be targeting specific times and locations where your target audience is more likely to be there.

HOWEVER, working in a truck or trailer comes with limited space. Compared to a fixed location, this venture limits the range of services you can provide. Depending on your location, you may need a permit to operate your mobile business. Overall, it is a good choice for a start-up. But, eventually, you will need an upgrade.

ONLINE ADVERTISING

Almost everyone who wants to open a business uses digital marketing these days. This is an interactive form of advertisement that can help you get more customers. But, for this to work, you need a website.

A SURVEY SHOWS THAT 86% of marketers boosted their brand awareness by using one or multiple digital marketing strategies. Here are a couple of options to use.

EMAIL MARKETING ALLOWS you to engage with your potential clients. You can use it to provide updates on promotions, tips for knife maintenance, or exclusive sharpening offers. This is a cost-effective way to find and keep a steady client base.

FOR AN EVEN GREATER IMPACT, you can combine print advertising with e-mail marketing. Studies found that when using, email and print advertising, businesses notice an average of a 125% increase in inquiries and a 49% increase in sales.

Search engine advertising, like Google Ads, helps your business find clients who search for relevant keywords (e.g. "knife sharpening service near me"). This option gives you high visibility and better reach.

PLATFORMS LIKE INSTAGRAM, Facebook, and Twitter can help you connect with your audience. They give you the perfect opportunity to show before-and-after results or post video content where you can show your skills in action.

COMPELLING VIDEOS ARE MORE likely to have more views and be shared. This organic sharing creates traffic and exposure. When clients see their own knives being sharpened and packaged on social media, it creates a unique experience. It makes them feel appreciated and valued. You can use videos to highlight every step that it takes to make a sharp knife and the care you put into each blade.

DISPLAY ADVERTISING IS another way to get more clients. For example, your ad can be featured on a website that does arts and crafts, gardening content, or food forums. Schedule your ads to appear during peak hours when your target audience is more likely to browse these websites.

WORD-OF-MOUTH MARKETING

Another really great strategy that you can focus on is word-of-mouth marketing. Now, you have to understand that there is no way to actually push this. It rather comes down to how you serve your customers. The good news is that word-of-mouth marketing is completely free and can really help to establish trust and authority for you in the local community.

FIRST, let's consider how word-of-mouth marketing works. When you deliver a really great service to a customer, and they are happy with your business, they're more likely to actually recommend you to people they know. The thing is, people are more likely to trust a brand when someone they know recommends it.

. . .

THIS IS why it's important to ensure you offer your customers a friendly service. Make sure to sharpen their knives the right way and go the extra mile. That's going to help establish trust, which helps to increase the chances of getting recommendations. When you take the effort to really focus on the customer's experience, you're not only going to benefit from word-of-mouth marketing. Building trust helps to create returning customers as well.

BUILDING A LOYAL CUSTOMER BASE

Now that we've taken a look at why it's so important to market your business and even shared a couple of promotional strategies, it's time that we start focusing on how you can actually build loyalty among your customers. The thing is - when you run a business, especially with a local company, you want to create trust among the people who use your services.

WHILE IT'S REALLY useful to get new customers in on a regular basis, you have to also understand the value that existing clients can bring to your business. Nurturing the existing clients can help you with two things. First, it's going to get those customers to continue using your business. Even if you do a really good job of sharpening their knives, there comes a time when they'll need to get these blades sharpened again.

MAYBE A CUSTOMER DECIDES to test your services by bringing you one set of knives, but they have more at home. If you're able to sharpen their knives to or beyond their expectations, they're likely going to bring you more sets. You're essentially going to start establishing yourself as an authority within the sharpening niche, particularly in the community that you're a part of.

COMMON LEAD GENERATION MISTAKES TO AVOID

Lead generation is incredibly important when it comes to running a business. A lead is when a customer comes to you and asks you about the pricing of your services and what you can offer them. This could be in the form of an email, phone call, or someone coming in to see you. At this point, it's up to you to convert the lead into a customer.

Now, there are actually a couple of common mistakes that people make when they work on lead generation and marketing campaigns. By knowing more about these mistakes, it's easier to ensure you don't fall into the same traps. Instead, you can learn from mistakes that others have made. That's going to help you prevent problems and make your campaigns more efficient.

Let's take a closer look at a couple of these mistakes that you should avoid:

- **Not following up:** If you receive an email or a query regarding your services, consider the person a lead. Now, one mistake to avoid is to not follow up. Sometimes, the person checks in with you to see what you can offer them, and your response sits in their inbox. They may just need a little "nudge" to actually reach out and use your services. Give it a few days, and if they don't respond, do a quick follow up. Don't try to push your services off on them, but rather just ask them if they have any more questions.
- **Call to action:** When someone lands on your website or perhaps see an ad for your business in a local newspaper, they are generally looking for what is

known as a call to action. Telling people what you expect them to do can greatly increase the chances that they contact you. "Call me to get your knives sharpened", "Click here to schedule" - something like this shows a clear action that the person should take. Use a call to action whenever you set up promotional campaigns that are meant to help get you more leads.

- **Failure to be consistent:** Consistency is another important thing that plays a role in helping you get more leads. When you're not consistent, your marketing efforts start to go to waste. The idea here is to post advertisements or content regularly. If you run a Facebook page for your business, try to post at least a few times every week. Have a set schedule so that your audience knows when they can expect an update from you.
- **Not tracking performance:** ROI, or return on investment, is something that can help you understand the viability and overall performance of your marketing and lead generation campaigns. You have to keep track of how many leads you get with each of the lead generation strategies that you use. This can help you determine how much you spend and what you get in return. If you're not tracking this, then you could be spending way too much money on marketing campaigns. The data you collect when tracking the performance of your campaigns can also help you optimize future strategies that you use.
- **Giving up:** This is one mistake that a lot of people are guilty of. Giving up too soon. When you set up a campaign to help you collect more leads and ultimately convert them into paying customers, there might be times when the results you get seem poor. Deciding to give up without allowing the campaign to run for a bit can be a bad idea. It often takes a while

for these campaigns to really take off and give you the results you expect.

Summary / *Key Takeaways*

- Your business is really nothing without customers. You need to adopt the right marketing strategies to get people to contact you for your services.
- There are different marketing techniques that you can use, both online and offline.
- Attend a local farmer's market, join local communities, set up an online presence for your business, and offer mobile services. These are all great ways to find customers that can make use of your services.
- Apart from understanding what marketing techniques you can use, it's also important to ensure you don't overlook some common lead-generation mistakes people make. Don't give up too quickly, make sure you track the progress of your campaigns, and be consistent with your strategies.

Now that you have a better understanding of how you can find paying clients for your sharpening business, it's time to look at what steps to take when you want to scale your business in the next chapter.

CHAPTER 10
SCALE YOUR BUSINESS

You've come a long way with your knife sharpening business. By now, you should know everything to get going. In the previous chapters, we focused on the initial steps to take, such as choosing a niche, setting up your workspace, and finding clients. As you continue to market your business and get customers to use your services, you may find that the demand for your service begins to increase.

PEOPLE MAY START to recommend your services to others. Your marketing campaigns have had time to run and you optimized them, so now they are also bringing in more leads and customers. At this point, it's important to understand what it means to actually scale your business.

WHEN YOUR KNIFE sharpening business is successful, think of scaling up as taking it to the next level. While some people may be comfortable with maintaining what they've built, extra income is always useful. Sometimes, you could even use scaling as a way to have your knife sharpening business completely replace that 9-to-5 job that you have to go through every day.

IN THIS CHAPTER, we're going to assess a couple of things that will help you determine if it's a good choice to scale up. That includes the pros and cons of scaling your business, and what you should expect. We're also going to look at specific signs that show you are at the right point to take your business up a level. This way, you won't make a mistake like scaling up when it's not time yet, or taking the wrong steps.

SHOULD YOU SCALE?

Before you really go into the entire process of scaling your business, you first have to consider two important things. First, you'll need to do some thinking and consider whether you actually want to scale the business. Secondly, you have to look at statistical reports and see how you're performing, as there are some criteria you should ideally create for yourself.

BEFORE YOU BEGIN SCALING, you should make sure your business meets this set of criteria.

OF COURSE, it's important to understand that scaling up is not for everyone. There are entrepreneurs who would grab the opportunity by hand when they can scale up. However, if your knife sharpening business is more of a hobby or something that you just do on the side, you might want it to stay that way. In such a case, you can actually skip over this chapter. But, if there's a chance that you might like to expand and level up your business, then be sure to stick around.

. . .

To HELP you get a better idea of what scaling means and the things you should expect, we're going to take a quick look at the benefits and possible disadvantages. These pros and cons can tell you a lot about the process itself.

PROS:

- When you scale up, your ability to serve customers expands. That means you'll be able to take orders from more customers than before.
- By offering your services to more people and taking in larger batches of work, it also means you'll be making more money with your business.
- Depending on how you do the scaling, it's sometimes possible to even step away and have others handle things for a while. That can give you time to spend with your family, friends, on hobbies, and other things that you usually don't get to.
- While you're going to be accepting more orders, when you scale up, it's also possible to use a couple of strategies that can actually reduce your overall workload.

CONS:

- It takes a significant amount of work and effort from your side to scale up. Sure, over time, your workload can actually decrease, but during the earlier stages of scaling, you're going to have a lot on your plate.

- Stress is another drawback that comes with scaling up. Whether you're working a day job or starting your own business, stress has become something that we just can't avoid in the modern day. However, when you choose to scale up, the steps you have to take can be stressful. There are also consistent worries about the risk that you are taking.
- You will need to hire people if you plan on expanding and scaling up. That means you're going to take a risk with your employees. If you can't find the right people for the job, it can have a serious impact on your ability to scale the business up.

SCALING YOUR BUSINESS

IF YOU DECIDE to scale up, then it's time to sit down and strategize. Creating a solid strategy will be incredibly helpful when it comes to scaling up your business. You'll basically have documents to go on, and a strategy that you can fall back to whenever you feel unsure about anything.

Now, it's important to understand that there are actually a couple of different ways to scale your business. It really comes down to the type of knife sharpening business you've built and the progress you've made. Personal preference will also play a crucial role when it comes to deciding how you want to scale your business.

SINCE THERE ARE SO many different options that you can consider when you take your business to the next level, we're going to take a closer look at a couple of examples. Note that this doesn't mean you can only choose one of these. Instead, most people will actually choose a combination of these strategies to help them push their business to new heights.

- **Expanding your services:** One of the easiest and simplest ways to really scale up is by introducing new services to what you are already offering. Maybe you started out by just offering your clients access to knife sharpening services. You also placed limitations on the specific types of knives, perhaps stating that you only deal with standard kitchen knives. Now, as demand for your services grow, you often get clients who require other types of knives sharpened. You can use this as an opportunity to scale up - and expand into these knife types. It's a basic start, but you can now continue to expand your services over time.
- **Expand locations:** Maybe you decided to begin your business from home. As you get more clients, your profit starts to increase. At some point, you might be able to afford renting a local business building and offer your services there. This can be an excellent way to spread more awareness of your business and increase your client count.
- **Hire staff:** You can also choose to hire some staff members to help out with different tasks. Tackling everything on your own is fine at the beginning, but as the business grows, you're going to need more hands. By hiring people, you'll be able to get another one on the sharpening stone. This will increase your capacity and make sure you can now sharpen double the number of knives at the same time. A receptionist or assistant can also be useful, as they can handle things like answering calls, responding to emails, sending out invoices, and other administrative tasks.

START small when expanding and take things step by step. That way, you won't have big expenses that suddenly fall onto you, which can take a toll on your business. Even if things are going really well, be careful about the decisions you make and how fast you go through the scaling process.

7 STEPS FOR SCALING YOUR BUSINESS

Now that we've looked at a few options that you could consider when you want to scale up your business, it's time to review the steps you should take. We've been going through a step-by-step system to help you understand how to start your knife sharpening business thus far. Now, we're also going to focus on a basic seven-step process that you can use to make sure you scale up effectively.

STEP 1: Define your goals
To be efficient in expanding your business, you have to know what you want to achieve throughout the process. That's where goals come into the picture. When you first started your knife sharpening business, you already defined some specific goals that you can strive toward. Now, as you are planning to scale your business, it's time to revisit those goals, and create new ones.

WHY DO you want to scale up your business? And what do you expect to achieve through scaling?

THESE ARE two important questions that you have to answer in order to create a good foundation which you can work from.

94

Maybe you want to scale up because the workload is getting more than you can handle, and hiring someone to help you out feels like a good idea. Or, perhaps you feel that by expanding, you can really push up the profits you bring home with the services you offer. Now, you can use this information to help you identify the specific goals that you want to strive for when scaling your knife sharpening business.

STEP 2: Analyze your current situation

There are a couple of things to do before you begin the actual scaling process. Apart from setting your goals, you also have to understand the situation your business is in right now. That means analyzing everything. Draw up reports to see how many clients you have, the number of blades you sharpen on average every day, how much money you are making, adn what your expenses look like You have to be realistic and understand whether or not scaling up is actually something that you can afford to do at this point.

STEP 3: Find your growth potential

Once you have a good overview of where you're standing with your business right now, it's time to look at the potential for growth that exists. Now, you're just starting with expansions for your business, so at the time, you have to try to keep things simple and easy. Look for growth opportunities that are easy to go for instead of ones that require a lot of complicated stops.

It's a good idea to take a look at the market and your community. You can often find "clues" for growth opportunities, such as new services that could land you additional customers. For example, ask customers if they have any other blades that they need to be sharpened. If you can't help them with those blades, it presents an opportunity for growth.

It's ALSO useful to determine if you want to opt for a vertical or horizontal scaling plan. Basically, do you want to get more customers for a specific service that you offer? Or do you rather want to offer more services to your customers? That's an important thing to keep in mind.

STEP 4: Develop a scaling plan

Now that you have a better idea of what you expect from the scaling process, it's important to develop a plan. Open up a document on your computer or get a piece of paper. Documenting everything makes sure you have a plan to follow.

THE PLAN WILL BE personal - as it's based on the decisions that you've made. You have to outline the specific steps that you need to take in order to make this scaling process a reality. If you want to offer more services, for example, the steps may include getting new equipment, training yourself, and customizing your marketing strategies.

IF YOU'RE HAVING TROUBLE, consult online guides or perhaps talk to some local business owners. Chances are, there are local businesses that have scaled up in the past. Ask them about the plans they used to level up their business. Even just a couple of tips can help you out. Another option is to search for a template that you can use. This can give you some structure as a foundation to help you develop a good plan.

· · ·

WHILE YOU'RE WORKING on this scaling plan, make sure to keep everything well-structured. The document should look professional and clean. That way, you won't find yourself scrolling through unnecessary information when the time comes to actually take action.

STEP 5: Implement your plan

Once you have a plan that's detailed and well-structured, it's time to put it into action. Remember that during the previous step, you created a specific flow that you have to follow. So, start at the very beginning. That might include buying a new piece of hardware, for example.

GO SLOW and don't try to push things. If you take it too fast, then you might run into problems or even feel overwhelmed when things start to get too much. Just take it day-by-day and don't expect to see massive results overnight. When you go at this slow pace, you give yourself a chance to adapt as you make changes to your business.

IF YOUR PLAN includes hiring other people, make sure you set aside some time to do interviews with them. The main thing here is to spend time with every person who applies for the position. If you're not used to the entire hiring process, then it's often difficult to know which applicant is the right fit. Take a look at the resumes you are sent, but also conduct personal interviews to see who you'll be working with.

THEN, as you go through these interviews, you can see which of the applicants are the better fit for a specific position that needs to be filled. For example, someone who has worked as a receptionist, personal assistant, or office administrator in the past might be a great fit to get things organized.

Step 6: Monitor your progress

After you implement the necessary steps to put your plan into action, it's important that you continuously track and monitor. The thing is, if you don't keep an eye on how the plan is coming along, it's hard to know whether it's worth it. Set up the right tools that can give you an easy view of what's going on and how everything is working out.

You could use an online system that tracks sales and customers, for example. When you draw reports from this system, you can see whether your sales and customer count have been increasing as you've implemented your plans to scale up. You also have to see if your profits are actually increasing.

When you monitor the progress, you can also see if it's worth it. Now, there might come a time when you find progress to be slow or even not getting anywhere close to the goals you have set. That doesn't mean your scaling plan isn't working. Either your plan needs to be tweaked a little, or perhaps you are not giving it enough time yet. It takes some time for everything to fall into place, especially if the expansion of your business has some extra expenses that you have to cover.

It's a good idea to use different types of monitoring and assessment systems. That's going to help give you a more significant amount of data to work with. And when it comes to making big decisions in business work, the more data you have, the better. Integrated systems can also be very useful here, as they'll usually give you multiple tools in a single platform - for example, this type of system could provide reports on customers, returning customers, income, expenses, and more.

STEP 7: Adjust your plan as needed

As you monitor the progress of your plan and expansion, you have to regularly sit down with the reports. It's not just about monitoring. You also have to understand if there are any areas in your plan or actions you've taken that need to change. Sometimes, we create a plan, and it looks great, but even when we plan for the future, there are things that can change. That's because the future isn't always predictable.

So, with this in mind, if you find any specific points in your progress reports that seems like there is an area not performing well - that needs to be addressed. For example, maybe you've introduced a new service, have several clients, but they're not returning. Go back to the actual service you're offering. Maybe the customers aren't as happy as they should be. In such a case, review the process you use to sharpen their blades. Perhaps the fault lies with the equipment or the specific technique that you've been using.

ANOTHER EXAMPLE COULD BE that productivity is limited because you have a small workspace. So, even while you're offering more services to your customers and you are getting more orders for your service, you're having a difficult time working alongside another employee - when both of you are working on sharpening these blades. In this case, you could consider expanding the size and layout of your workspace. Alternatively, you can look for a bigger building to rent - but you'll have to make sure that the monthly rental fees are still a good fit for your budget.

. . .

SUMMARY / *Key Takeaways*

- Scaling up can be great for business, but you also have to understand that it's not for everyone. Keep your personal preferences in mind to help you decide if it's something that you see yourself doing for your sharpening business.
- When you decide to scale up, you have to use criteria to help you determine when it's time to take these steps.
- A simple seven-step system can make the scaling-up process easier and less stressful. However, you still need to weigh the pros and cons of this decision against each other.

YOU'VE NOW BEEN GIVEN a solid seven-step system that you can use to not only start your own knife sharpening business, but also to grow it. We've gone through every step in detail, and you should now be ready to take action. However, there are still a couple of other things that we should still cover, starting at numbers. In the next chapter, we'll talk a bit more about finances and how you can keep track of everything.

CHAPTER II

CHOPPING UP THE NUMBERS

Running a knife sharpening business involves more than just sharpening knives and other blades that customers bring to you. Failure to keep up with the numbers is one of the biggest mistakes you can make. You need to understand how profitable your business is and, of course, use your financial sheets to stay in line with the laws. You see, there are taxes that you need to pay - and if your finances are not in order, you're going to have a tough time ensuring everything works out.

YOU DON'T NECESSARILY NEED to be a financial expert when it comes to working with finances. However, it's definitely a good idea to take a quick online course to give you a headstart when it comes to your finances. Additionally, it's also important to consider using an online system that can help streamline the process.

THERE ARE cloud-based systems that can be very useful in this particular case. These systems are designed to give you easy and quick access to your most vital data at any time. They can be accessed from your smartphone, laptop, and tablet. Our focus here is not only on helping you pick a good system but rather on giving you an overview of the factors you have to cover to manage your business - on the financial level.

However, it's important to decide on a system that's going to comply with the needs of your own business. You're beginning a knife sharpening business, which means you don't need an enterprise-grade system. There are even free options that you can use. Some of these systems let you get started for free, and then upgrade when needed.

The reason we recommend using an online system is because it really simplifies things. Look for a system that lets you add details of your customers, and generate invoices, and one that gives you a chance to actually load up expenses too. This type of system will let you easily get details about your clients, see which ones are continuously using your services, and can give you access to the resources you need to analyze the efficacy of your business operations.

Throughout this chapter, we're going to talk about the break-even point. That's one of the first things you have to determine when it comes to making money with your knife sharpening business. We'll also take a look at specific performance metrics you should not overlook and talk a bit about paying taxes and staying in line with the legal aspects of business management.

CALCULATING YOUR BREAK-EVEN POINT

Let's start with the break-even point. No matter what kind of business you want to start, you have to know your break-even point, and also understand why it's such an important figure.

DURING THE INITIAL steps you take to actually start your business, you're going to have some expenses. Of course, the budget that you have to begin with will decide how much those expenses are going to be. The break-even point is essentially the "point" where you can say, "okay, I've covered my expenses, now I can start making a profit."

So, to get started with this process, you first have to understand the costs that you take on when starting this knife sharpening business. Write down the total costs.

A FEW EXAMPLES of expenses could include the sharpening stone that you will buy to actually sharpen blades. Maybe you also decide to buy a workbench, as that's going to make your life easier. A strop is another useful item in this type of business, as you'll be able to offer additional polishing services to your customers. Now, let's say all of these items come to a total of $200.

TO BREAK EVEN, you need to make $200 from the services you'll be offering your clients. The income from your clients will depend on a couple of things, such as the specific sharpening services they require. Let's assume that you can get a minimum profit of $5 per sale when someone just has a basic knife to sharpen. That's a bare minimum you can work with - and it means after selling this service 40 times, you'll get to a profit of $200 - which will be your break-even point.

ANY PROFIT that you make after the break even point is above the expenses that you had to undergo to get started. Working with a bare minimum per sale helps to keep things realistic. You might break even much faster, as that's only one service that you offer. Some clients may have multiple knives to sharpen, for example. This can increase your profit per sale, and ultimately help you reach the $200 faster.

PERFORMANCE METRICS TO WATCH

As you run your knife sharpening business, there are a couple of metrics that you should prioritize. By knowing what metrics are the most important, it gives you a chance to focus on things that really matter. You also won't find yourself wasting time analyzing specific metrics that aren't as important - or doesn't necessarily need to be monitored so frequently.

LET'S take a closer look at the specific metrics that you should focus on when you are running your knife sharpening business. The ability to keep an eye on these performance metrics is not only good in the short term, but can also become incredibly valuable in helping you decide when it's time to start thinking about scaling up your business.

- **Sales Volume:** Let's start with sales volume. Now, you're not actually selling a product with a knife sharpening business (except if you decide to sell knives and other supplies). That doesn't mean you can't track sales volume, as every service that someone needs you to perform (sharpening their knives, adding polishing), is a sale. When it comes to tracking your sales volume, it's important to keep an eye on your overall sales. At the same time, break things down into multiple categories too if you don't offer just one single service. For example, you could track sales for knife sharpening, polishing, and even sales for any products you offer your customers. This can give you an idea about specific products or services that are doing really well, while also allowing you to identify areas you need to focus on a bit more.

- **Revenue:** Knowing how much money you're actually bringing in with your sharpening services is critical. How else will you know if your business is actually profitable? Revenue refers to the total amount of money you are able to get in from all of the products and services you offer. Similar to sales volume, you can actually break this down into categories, and have one overall figure as well. The more in-depth you go with the details, the greater amount of data you will have to work with. You'll regularly refer back to your revenue data to get an idea of what works and what doesn't, as this can be incredibly helpful when it comes to making decisions going forward.

- **Cost of service:** Knowing how much it costs to deliver a specific service or provide a product to a customer is another important metric that you don't want to overlook. When it comes to the cost of sharpening a knife, this one can be quite tricky.

If you're not using a machine, but rather a manual sharpening stone, then you'll have to take its cost into account - but you're using the same stone for many knives. Instead, you need to consider how many knives you can sharpen with the stone. This does depend on the stone, as well as the technique you use. Stones tha thave a very coarse exterior can give you sharpening for a few hundred sharpenings. However, the finer stones can actually last for about 1500 sharpenings. Consider more or less how many times you can sharpen a blade on the stone, and divide its cost with that number.

Let's say you use a medium stone that can do about 1000 sharpenings, and you pay $200 for the stone. This would mean that every sharpening service you provide to your clients cost you about $0.20. There could be other expenses too, so take a closer look at your entire process.

In cases where you've decided to offer additional sale services, such as knives or even home-use sharpening tools, you'll have to consider your purchasing price. This is the amount you pay to actually buy these items from a vendor, which you will then resell to your customers.

- **Gross profit:** Now that you have an idea of your revenue and cost per good / service, you can actually start to look at your gross profit. Now, this is not yet your "take home" profit, as there are a couple of extra things that we're still going to take a look at. But, it's a good idea to still calculate your gross profit before you proceed.

TO GET YOUR GROSS PROFIT, you're basically going to take your revenue and deduct the cost per goods or services sold from it. Let's say in a one-month period you sharpen knives for 50 clients. The average order gets you $5, and the only cost to you is the sharpening stone. You'll have $250 in revenue and your cost is around $10, based on the previous calculation we used in the example. That leaves you with a gross profit of $240.

OF COURSE, it's important to keep in mind that these are all example figures and they will not be exactly the same for you. In order to be successful, you'll have to keep your specific data in mind when you are doing these calculations.

- **Operating expenses:** Now, when you run your knife sharpening business, there are going to be some operating expenses. At first, your operating expenses will likely be very low, but you should still ensure you don't skip this step.

YOUR OPERATING COSTS relate to what it cost you to actually keep the business running. This can include things like extra power that you're using, for example. Even if you don't use a machine to sharpen knives, consider the extra hours you now have the light on in the specific area. Maybe you bought additional lights to make sure you can closely inspect the knives. Other operational costs may include expenses related to marketing campaigns, software you use to keep your business organized, and perhaps additional supplies that you regularly stock up on.

You have to calculate your operating costs over a certain period of time. The period depends on the timeframe for the other expenses that you're calcuating. You might calculate everything every month, but also at each quater and then once again do an annual report.

- **Net profit:** Finally, with all of this data on hand, it's now possible for you to calculate your net profit. This is, as they call it, your "take home" profit. It's the amount of money you make after you've deducted the expenses that you have to undergo in order to run your knife sharpening business.

Start with your gross profit, then deduct your operating expenses. The final figTure - that's your net profit. Now, this doesn't mean you can just spend everything. When you've calculated your net profit, you're still going to have to pay your taxes. Plus, it's always a good idea to take some of the net profit you make and put it away. Open a savings account, for example. You can then use this money you save up as a way to help you expend your business later on.

PAYING TAXES

The one part that self-employed people often dread - taxes. Many employers actually deducts taxes from employee salaries automatically, which makes it easier for the average person to ensure their taxes are paid. If you're self-employed, such as in this case where you're opening your own sharpening business, then you have to actually report and pay taxes on your own.

THERE ARE a couple of ways to go about this process. If you're not used to paying taxes yourself, however, then it might be a good idea to contact an agency that works with this type of thing. When it comes to taxes, there are two types that you'll need to file for when you're running your own sharpening business. These include income tax, as well as Social Security tax.

THE IRS DEMANDS that you file a quarterly return. Every quarter, you'll use your financial data to make a prediction for how much you're going to earn throughout the year. You'll then be paying your taxes based on the prediction. By the end of the financial year, you'll submit another report with accurate data that reflects on your statements - the IRS can then determine if there is a refund due to you or if you still need to pay in any extra fees.

ONE THING TO keep in mind is that if you don't pay enough taxes during the year, then by the end of the period, you might get extra penalty fees added to your taxes. That's one of the reasons why it's really useful to get an agency to help you manage your taxes.

A PROFESSIONAL WITH experience understands how the entier process works. They can also give you expert advice and guide you throughout the process.

. . .

IN ADDITION TO THESE STRATEGIES, you should also consider setting up an LLC. This is a limited liability corporation, and it can actually help to give you certain tax-related benefits. A tax professional can guide you through the process, as well as help you weigh the pros and cons of this decision.

OF COURSE, the tax-related data that we looked at now focuses on the United States. Every country has its own specific rules and regulations to follow when it comes to paying taxes. The specific institution that deals with tax collection also differs between various countries. Thus, if you're not in the United States, then things will likely be at least somewhat different in your country. Reach out to your local tax authorities to learn more about how they handle self-employed tax payers and what procedures you should follow to get started.

SUMMARY / *Key Takeaways*

- You have to keep on top of your finances to ensure the success of your sharpening business. This starts with regularly checking reports and knowing what performance metrics play a big role.
- When you regularly assess these reports, you'll get a better idea about how your business is doing. You can then use this data to make important decisions going forward.
- Apart from understanding how to calculate your expenses and profit, you shouldn't overlook the responsibility that now falls onto you to pay taxes. If you're having difficult with taxes, then talk to an expert to get some insight and help.

IN THIS CHAPTER, you found out why it's so important to keep track of finances related to your knife sharpening business. We addressed important metrics too. In the next chapter, we're shifting our attention to some mistakes that people often make when they start their own knife sharpening business. These mistakes can be costly, so learning more about them can make sure you don't fall into them yourself - thus reducing the risk of mistakes that could ruin your ability to be successful.

CHAPTER 12
MISTAKES TO AVOID

You should have an idea about how great a knife sharpening business can be. We've gone through the steps you have to take, as well as considered ways to get customers, and even talked about expanding your business. Now, it's important to understand that there are other people who have started a knife sharpening business before you. And it's not just about this specific type of business. People start businesses on a daily basis, and they often make mistakes.

WHEN YOU KNOW what mistakes people tend to make, then it's easier to ensure you don't make them yourself. It can really help to make your business be more functional and successful, as you won't find yourself in pitfalls as others have before you. This chapter is entirely dedicated to some of these common mistakes that people tend to make when they start and run a small business.

BUSINESS-BUILDING MISTAKES TO AVOID

There are a lot of mistakes that we tend to make when starting a business. This especially accounts for cases where you don't really have previous experience with running a business and related tasks. So, let's take a closer look at a couple of mistakes that are really common, but often overlooked - especially by beginners.

TRYING to compete with pricing

One big mistake that I see a lot of people make is trying to compete on price. Competitor research is really important when it comes to starting your own business. One of your main goals here is to find ways to "outshine" the competition and get people to choose your business instead of them.

A COMMON WAY for people to do this is to try and be the cheapest in town. Sure, a lower price can attract customers, but it's also going to make your business look cheap. You have to assess the quality of the services your competitors offer, and compare this to their pricing. Then, consider your own skill and the equipment you're using. You need to set competitive prices, not the cheapest prices in the local area.

NOT MARKETING your business

What's the use of having the best skills in town and offering the highest quality service, when nobody knows about your business? One of the biggest mistakes you can make is not promoting your business. Sure, telling a few people about the services you're going to offer is a good start, but that's not enough to make sure you're going to have a consistent stream of customers.

. . .

You have to go out there and spread the word. That means putting up posters where applicable (yes, posters are still a great idea for this kind of business). You can also place ads in local newspapers and see if your local radio stations are open for some collaboration. Online advertisements is also great. The idea is to make sure people who are in need of your services can easily identify your business and get ahold of your contact details.

Failing to keep up with technology

When you're sharpening knives as a service, then you might not think much of technology. However, failure to keep up with the latest tech advances can leave you falling behind. This includes following trends of how people are promoting their businesses on social media, for example. Even small local businesses are taking to TikTok, Facebook, Twitter, and other social networks to spread the word. It's a great way to really connect with your audience and grow a fanbase.

Apart from this, there are also technological advancements in terms of hardware that people use to sharpen knives. Keeping up with these innovations gives you a chance to bring the latest things into your workplace. In turn, your business operations would be more efficient.

Technology also extends to the use of digital systems that helps you manage your business properly.

Not getting the right insurance

Insurance is really important when it comes to creating your own business. You may not think much of insurance when it comes to a knife sharpening business, but what if a client brings you a really expensive knife set and you accedentally damage it? You're going to need to replace their knives.

FINDING a good insurance plan can be very helpful if you ever find yourself in these situatinos.

NOT KNOWING **your costs**

When you're just getting started, you might not take down information about all of the expenses you make to actually run the business. Sure, you note down the money you paid for the sharpening stone, but that's not the only expense you're going to have to cover.

WHAT ABOUT THINGS like the gas you use to go from place to place? The amount of money you spend on Facebook Ads? Electricity cost for machines and lighting you use in your workspace? These are all things that we easily overlook, and if you don't have a clear view of all your expenses, it's hard to really know how your business is doing.

NOT PLANNING **for slow periods**

No matter what kind of business you run, there are always going to be times when things seem slow. This could be at the beginning even for some people. Then, you get a period where things pick up, followed by a slow pace again.

THE THING IS, it's normal to have slow periods. However, if you're not prepared for them and know how to estimate when it might happen, then it can leave you in the dark. Once you enter the slow period, motivation suddenly seems like a stranger to you. And once your motivation starts to fall, you may start to think that your business is beginning to fail.

INSTEAD, you should be resilient and equip yourself with the ability to understand that it's just a slow period. Decide how you're going to address these periods beforehand, as that's going to help you feel more prepared.

FAILING to comply with regulations

There are certain regulations that you have to comply with when running a business. If you're not in compliance with these regulations, you could find yourself in trouble down the line.

IT'S a good idea to contact your local government authorities when you start planning your knife sharpening business. Ask them about specific regulations that will apply to this specific type of business. It may include applying for a license, for example. While on the subject of complying with regulations, it's also important to ensure you understand how taxes work and pay them on time.

NOT KEEPING good records

Record keeping is definitely not something for everyone. There are those who are really good at keeping a record of everything. If you're not keeping records of everything, then it could spell trouble for you in the long run.

. . .

THE IDEA here is to keep a record of everything related to your business. That doesn't just include the invoices you send to your clients and the payments they make to you. It's important that you also keep receipts, for example. Whenever you go out to buy something for your business, place the receipt inside a file that you can reference later. This will give you more data to work with when you are assessing your business and trying to figure areas where you can make improvements.

SUMMARY / *Key Takeaways*

- There are several mistakes that people tend to make when it comes to starting a knife sharpening business. You have to learn more about these mistakes and then implement steps that will make sure you avoid them in your own journey.
- Some of the most common mistakes include not keeping records, not understanding your actual costs, and failure to market your business properly.

THESE ARE all important mistakes that you want to avoid when it comes to running a successful knife sharpening business. You'll have to start learning about them even before you start your business. Next, we're going to take a closer look at some case studies of real people who decided to start their own knife sharpening business.

CHAPTER 13

SUCCESS STORIES

As our journey throughout this book comes to an end, there's one more chapter that I want us to cover - success stories. You see, when it comes to starting a business of any kind, just the idea of the process itself can feel overwhelming. You're never guaranteed success. But, there's one thing that you can do to find motivation, and that's to read about the success of others.

AFTER SOME RESEARCH, I've found that there are a couple of success stories for people who wanted to start their own knife sharpening business. Taking a closer look at these stories can be a big help when it comes to giving you the inspiration you need to take the first step. And, if you ever come to a point where things feel like it's not working out, come back to these success stories. Read through them. Find inspiration in the successes that other people have been able to attain in this kind of market.

KNIFE AID

First up is Knife AId. Now, this knife sharpening business was actually started by two people. They are known as Marc Lickfett and Mikael Soderlind. The business was started in January 2019. Now, something to keep in mind is that they had a very unique element to their business model. Instead of having people bring their knives over, they instead started a business with a mail-in service structure.

CUSTOMERS WOULD MAIL their knives to the business to have them sharpened. The two would then sharpen the knives and return them to the respective owners by mail. In just one year, they were able to get to $250,000 in revenue per month. That's a massive growth in just 12 months! Following the massive success of Lickfett and Soderlind, the two even appeared on Shark Tank and they have since gained the attention of many investors.

BIANCO BROTHERS INSTRUMENTS

Bianco Brothers Instruments is an excellent example of the fact that a knife sharpening business can last for a very long time. In fact, the business was first founded in 1972. John Bianco, the initial founder of the business, actually bought a knife sharpening services from someone else back in the day. He then decided to dig into this type of business himself, and the business has been passed on to his son.

OVER THE YEARS, Bianco Brothers Instruments have grown tremendously. They now offer sharpening services for a diverse selection of blades. Additionally, they are also now manufacturers or certain tools.

AMERICAN EDGE SHARPENING

Another great example comes from a Naval Captain who decided to start a knife sharpening business part-time. He decided to call his business American Edge Sharpening, and he actually didn't have significant experience before starting the venture. In fact, he learned a lot of the skills he now has from watching videos on YouTube.

To FIND CUSTOMERS, the owner of American Edge Sharpening actually started with Facebook. He also did some local marketing within the community he stayed at. This allowed him to get some initial clients, and then he started to expand from there. It remains a part-time business for the owner, but he makes up to $60 per hour sharpening knives, which definitely isn't a bad rate.

THE SHARPEST KNIFE ON THE BLOCK

This story is truly inspirational and really shows that anyone can start a knife sharpening business. James Peggs watched his grandpa sharpen knives and equipped himeself with these skills. By the age of 13, Peggs decided to start offering knife sharpening services to other people in his local community. He simply wanted to earn some money to buy things for himself.

Now, this all happened when the world was in a pandemic (The Covid pandemic, of course). Peggs was able to buy some initial equipment to get started and got his first clients. Since then, he's actually been expanding, offering services that sharpens more than just your average kitchen knives. He also sharpens hatches, scissors, and chainsaws as part of his business now.

· · ·

A CONGRATULATIONS IS CERTAINLY in order. You've made it until the end, and hopefully feel more confident about actually starting your very own knife sharpening business now!

CONCLUSION

American Edge Sharpening started with just one guy and a dream. While he still remains the sole owner, the business has been thriving. The Sharpest Knife on the Block, started by a 13-year-old, is another great example of how a sharpening business can be a great business venture.

Throughout this book, we looked at important elements that can help you start your very own knife sharpening business. Now, as we reach the conclusion, it's time for you to take action. Delaying and procrastinating are things that you have to avoid now. You've shown your interest in starting this kind of businesss, so it's really important to take action. Even just small steps can help you achieve your dreams and build a successful shapening business.

The seven step system we shared is incredibly valuable and guides you through everything you need to know when starting this kind of business. It's important to follow it step-by-step. That means you need to start by establishing a niche that you're going to target, and then define your services. It's also important to know your prices and to create a decent workspace before you start offering your services to clients. Knowing when to scale up is another important point that you shouldn't overlook. When your business grows to a certain extend, it's time to consider whether or not you want to expand - and even simple steps like offering more services could have a substantial impact on your profits.

Now, it's over to you. Start small, but dream big. Set goals and follow up on them. Don't just focus on that long-term goal, but break it down so that it's easier to celebrate smaller achievements to keep yourself motivated.

REFERENCES & RESOURCES

- https://www.researchandmarkets.com/reports/5165400/u-s-knife-sharpening-service-market-size-share
- https://www.starterstory.com/ideas/sharpening-service/success-stories
- https://ph.rs-online.com/web/content/discovery/ideas-and-advice/sharpening-stones-guide
- https://www.nortonabrasives.com/en-us/resources/expertise/choosing-sharpening-stone
- https://www.masterclass.com/articles/the-best-ways-to-sharpen-a-knife-everything-you-need-to-know-about-knife-sharpening-and-benefits-of-a-sharp-kitchen-knife
- https://support.wickededgeusa.com/portal/en/kb/articles/how-often-do-you-need-to-replace-the-stones-is-there-a-certain-number-of-knifes-that-it-will-do
- https://www.dictum.com/en/blog/tool-knowledge/sharpening-tools-5-methods-for-sharpening-knives

- https://www.sba.gov/business-guide/plan-your-business/write-your-business-plan
- https://www.irs.gov/businesses/small-businesses-self-employed/self-employed-individuals-tax-center
- https://www.usatoday.com/story/entertainment/tv/2019/10/21/shark-tank-hungry-sharks-circle-around-knife-sharpening-business/4048496002/
- https://www.npr.org/2020/09/04/909154228/keeping-the-odd-family-tool-business-sharp-through-3-generations
- https://www.sidehustlenation.com/start-a-knife-sharpening-business/
- https://london.ctvnews.ca/making-the-cut-13-year-old-london-boy-starts-knife-sharpening-business-1.5036543

www.ingramcontent.com/pod-product-compliance
Lightning Source LLC
Chambersburg PA
CBHW071156290526

45796CB00007B/56